I0824972

At home with Blue

COMFORTABLE COUNTRY Enrica Stabile
CREATING A BEAUTIFUL HOME
ALEXANDRA STODDARD
Pretty Pastel Style
Selina Lake

At home with Blue

SOOTHING SPACES FOR RESTFUL LIVING

FIFI O'NEILL

Photography by **MARK LOHMAN**

CICO BOOKS

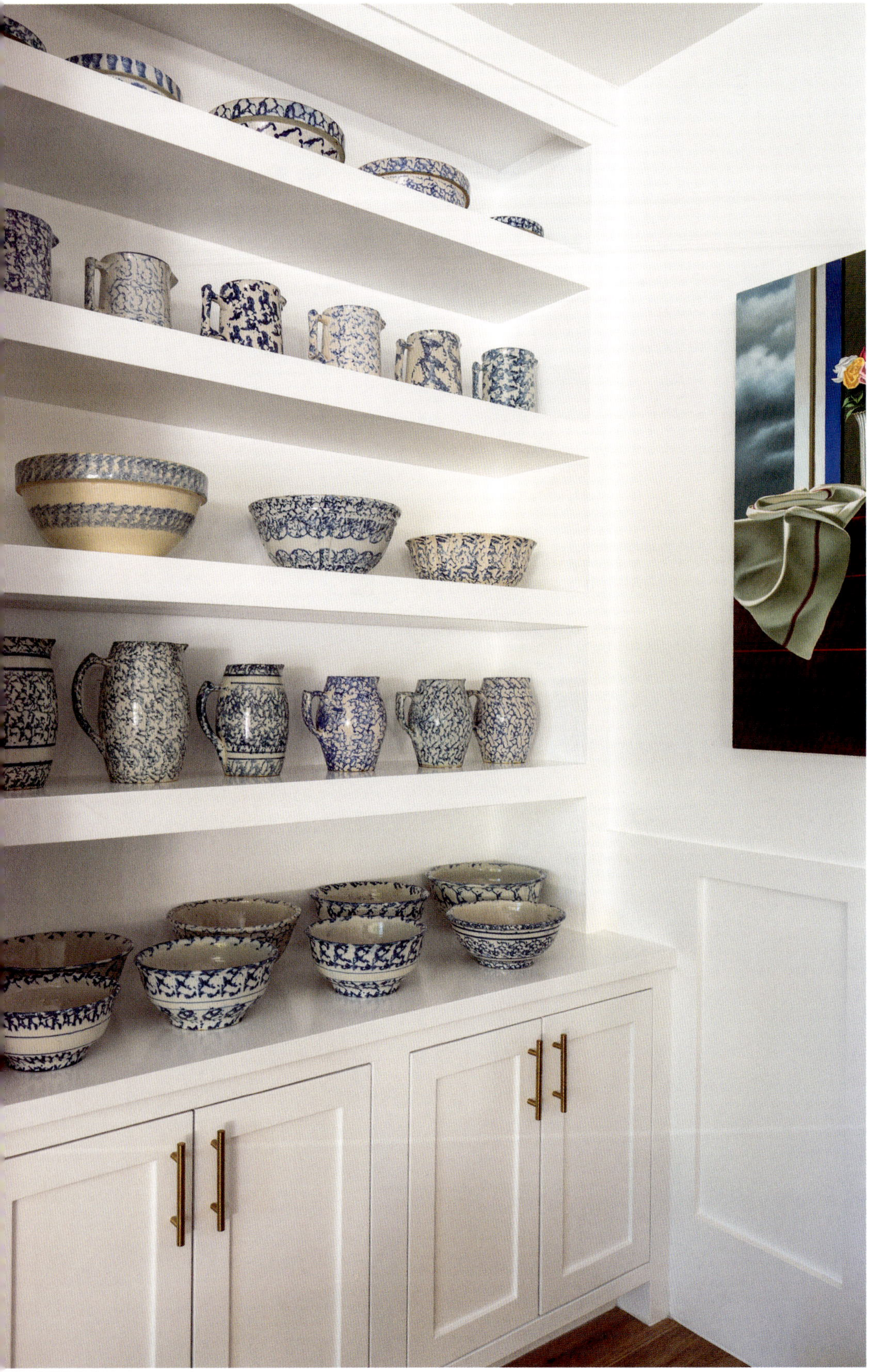

Senior designer Toni Kay
Editor Sophie Devlin
Production manager Gordana Simakovic
Senior commissioning editor
Annabel Morgan
Art director Sally Powell
Creative director Leslie Harrington

Published in 2026 by CICO Books.
An imprint of
Ryland Peters & Small
20–21 Jockey's Fields
London WC1R 4BW
and
1452 Davis Bugg Road
Warrenton, NC 27589
www.rylandpeters.com
Email: euregulations@rylandpeters.com

For photography credits and copyright information, see page 172.

10 9 8 7 6 5 4 3 2 1

ISBN 978-1-80065-460-0

A CIP record for this book is available from the British Library.

Library of Congress CIP data has been applied for.

Printed and bound in China

The authorized representative in the EEA is Authorised Rep Compliance Ltd., Ground Floor, 71 Lower Baggot Street, Dublin, D02 P593, Ireland
www.arccompliance.com

CONTENTS

"Blue is the only color that maintains its own character in all its tones. It will always stay blue."

Raoul Dufy (1877-1953), French painter

INTRODUCTION

From azure to cerulean, cobalt, indigo, sapphire, teal and turquoise to ultramarine, aquamarine and more, the vast spectrum of blues offers countless possibilities. This enchanting color effortlessly elevates the aesthetic of any room and is beloved for its calm, serene, tranquil and restorative qualities.

Blues are right at home in any room, whether your style skews country or urban, modern or classic, simple or sophisticated. It continues to be a beloved color choice for interiors, and for good reasons. From dreamy seaside hues to vibrant indigo, it's soothing while being sophisticated. A pale blue will soften a corner, whereas a deep blue brings a strong, regal touch and a bright blue adds a lively pop of color.

One of the many charms of blue is its versatility, as the 12 homes featured in this book amply demonstrate. They are arranged in four chapters, each presenting a different aspect of this much-loved color: Heavenly Blues, True Blues, Moody Blues and Atmospheric Blues. The owners of these homes have integrated their favorite blues into a variety of color palettes, reflecting the sea and sky but also evoking their treasured memories and expressing their creativity. Decorating trends may come and go, but we can always feel *At Home with Blue*.

INSPIRATIONS

PARIS

FABRICS

Blue fabrics come in infinite variations on the beloved color and a multitude of textures and patterns. Natural fibers such as cotton, linen, wool and silk can be finely woven for a smooth finish or embraced with all their imperfections. Deep-pile velvets and chenilles bring a rich softness to more sophisticated schemes. Whether mixing hues or favoring just one, materials play an important role in making spaces feel curated. Patterns also contribute a significant part in setting a mood by influencing visual perception, evoking emotions and creating an atmosphere. Be it in a sleek and contemporary home, a relaxed beach retreat, a sophisticated townhouse or a coastal cottage, the beauty of fabrics is the ability to achieve a unified and aesthetically pleasing appearance. The right mix of textiles never fails to instill charm, style and timelessness in any room.

PRETTY & PRACTICAL

Interiors primarily take their design cues from the function of a room, but our decorative choices are also influenced by the desire to establish a preferred aesthetic. Velvety pillows and a fleece throw create a little touch of luxury and convey warmth and comfort in this cozy cottage bedroom (opposite). Elsewhere, a cotton pillow and blanket with blue-and-white stripes afford a youthful and organic feel to a child's bed (above left). Uniting fabrics from different origins but with similar textures and patterns makes it easy to mix and match deeper and lighter hues (above center). From the table runner to the dishes and napkins, a palette of aqua is inspired by visions of breaking waves and salty air, a mood that lends itself to laid-back seaside style (above right).

MAKE IT LAST

Depending on where and how they are used, some fabrics are more suitable than others. Soft but strong and easy to care for, cotton is loved for its versatility–from pillows to sheets, curtains and tablecloths (top left). Crafted from a tightly woven mix of cotton and linen, French striped mattress ticking remains a favorite to bring a European flavor to indoor and outdoor furniture alike (top right). Chairs upholstered with durable sateen will stand up to daily wear and tear, offering a good alternative to more delicate satin yet maintaining a silky appearance (left). Rustic vintage grain sacks made of hemp can be upcycled into all kinds of soft furnishings, such as this pillow (above).

SLEEP TIGHT

Embroidery sends a personal message on a small hand-stitched pillow (right). It rests on a bed enveloped in layers of pristine linens with delicate sky-blue details that convey feminine fancy. Sleepovers are often a highlight for children and setting up a comfortable yet practical room is key to their enjoyment (below). Camp-style beds outfitted with cotton throws and pillows have a vacation vibe. A wide-striped rug echoes the pattern of the coverlets and keeps the mood of the room cohesive. A small stool upholstered with a dainty blue-and-white floral fabric balances the casual patterns of the other textiles.

FURNITURE

Furniture is much more than about filling a space. It plays a crucial part in establishing the overall mood and functionality of a room and in creating aesthetic appeal. Furniture designs run the gamut of styles and materials, but when it comes to finishes, blue is favored for its capacity to transform a space from quiet to dramatic as well as adding depth and dimension. A single sofa, chair or dresser/chest of drawers can kick any room up a notch and evoke a preferred atmosphere—from historical and classic to modern and laid-back—while pairing pieces from various eras allows for a dynamic and layered look. Rather than buying everything new, consider repainting the furniture you have to fit your chosen blue palette. Mixing different hues generates interest, whereas maintaining a cohesive scheme creates a soothing atmosphere.

BLUE BELLES

Outdoor furnishings are very much at home on a poolside patio or by the beach, as their bright blue tones reflect the sky and water surrounding them (above left and right). Together, a vintage dresser/chest of drawers painted in the palest shade and decorative items in soft turquoise impart a cottage flavor to a bedroom corner (above center). Vintage pieces are tied together by their simple lines and harmonious mix of colors, which keep this room from being too feminine (opposite). White surfaces make a pleasing counterpoint for the darker blues. An ample armoire, painted in two shades of pale aqua for a touch of contrast, brings balance to the room. Wood and metal accents add texture, while the bold patterns of the rug and pillow offer graphic focal points.

GRANGE
4
5
9
10
14
15
20
25
30
35
34
40

FRESH VINTAGE

Wearing its original paint, an old tool-factory cabinet makes a beautiful contrast to a 1960s chair and a step-back cupboard refinished with chalk paint (opposite). Eras and styles come together seamlessly on a terrace, where seat cushions sporting timeless stripes are a perfect fit for a modern bench and a rustic trunk sits comfortably on a new rug (right). A gently weathered table has found a new purpose as a little credenza/sideboard in a dining room (far right). Painted a deep teal hue, the back of a tall, narrow hutch/dresser offers a canvas for a collection of pottery, while artwork featuring an array of blue-and-white tableware amplifies the effect (below). It harmonizes well with the warm, rustic furniture pieces set against the white paneling.

BREAD
MODEL BAKERY
THE COOK'S ATELIER

MATERIALS & FINISHES

Materials and finishes are fundamental in shaping the look and atmosphere of a room—they contribute to the color palette, texture and overall visual and sensory experience. Thoughtful choices will help you to create a cohesive, beautiful and practical space that reflects your personal style. When looking at the homes featured in this book, consider how the owners' chosen materials bring a sense of intrigue, harmony and unity. From textural wood to cool marble and from sleek metals to rugged stone, the beauty of materials and the sensations and sentiments they evoke are the foundation of an attractive and emotionally impactful setting. And the same material can have a very different effect depending on the surface finish. All these elements are powerful allies when it comes to transforming your home indoors and out, from bland to dynamic, and to imbue every room with unique personality and charm.

VARIATIONS ON A THEME
An antique turquoise enamel bread bin is a fitting companion for a bouquet of flowers (opposite). Its hue and glossy finish make a striking counterpoint to the island's gently distressed white, while the polished wooden stool balances the rusticity of the vintage elements. Due to variations inherent in different materials, the same shade adapts to the item on which it is applied. Here, a weathered painted metal bucket shows the passage of time with remnants of faded aqua dotting its finish (above left). The coarseness and uneven qualities of a wood cabinet deepen its color and reveal subtleties in shading (above center). And the patinated surface of the candlestick has a muted elegance that evokes a sense of antiquity (above right).

SUPPORTING CHARACTER

Materials have a direct impact in establishing a space's unique visual experience: consider the warmth of wood or the elegance of stone, for example. Appropriately set atop a filigree headboard, ordinary wire shaped into a word sends a gentle request for quiet (left). The charm of bricks and wood floors lies in their natural beauty and imperfections that exude authenticity and infuse a room with a feeling of permanence and comfort, whether in a traditional or a modern setting (below).

GOOD COMPANIONS

Though they are not united by common materials, each of the elements of the patio–iron daybed, wooden bench, concrete planter and brick surface–enhance each other and come together to create a harmonious and inviting setting (top left). With their imperfect textures, organic shapes and hue variations, recycled glass bottles offer a vintage charm and a handcrafted appeal, making them a favorite choice for a sustainable aesthetic (top right). The wave-tumbled smoothness and varied hues of seaglass fragments and beads conspire to create unique decorative accents beloved for their many shades of blue (above). Weathered vintage shutters and classic wicker bring texture and timelessness to a plain wall (right).

DETAILS & DISPLAYS

Small things can have a big impact, and carefully curated displays are a definitive illustration of this mantra. When it comes to making a house a home, your personal possessions are the elements that make the biggest difference. They have the ability to elevate and personalize a room by enhancing its aesthetic appeal and imbuing it with personality, history, character and warmth. An unexpected vignette is always intriguing, especially one arranged with taste and discernment. It's one thing to build a collection of items that you love, but quite another knowing how to showcase them and integrate them into spaces. Whether it's a series of ornamental oddities that you adore, or the results of a passion for collected pottery, vintage bottles, seashells or beautiful dishes, your treasured items should be displayed in your home for all to see.

GROUP THERAPY

A little vignette composed of disparate items within the same color family creates a cohesive backdrop for knives with mother-of-pearl handles displayed in a vintage tin (above left). A potted plant set in a new bowl placed in an antique iron French spittoon is a lovely example of how to arrange decorative pieces with character and personality (above center). An array of cobalt bottles in varied heights, sizes and shapes provides an opportunity to compose an eye-catching arrangement (above right). Creativity and imagination go hand-in-hand when incorporating items in unexpected and inspiring ways. This old bottle drying rack affixed to a wall has a practical and decorative purpose when used to display turquoise glass jars, seasonal flowers, fresh herbs and coffee mugs (opposite).

RACHEL KHOO
LITTLE FRENCH KITCHEN

UNITED FRONT

A collection of spongeware pottery is more than the sum of its parts when cleverly arranged on built-in shelves (opposite). Together with the white backdrop, the symmetry of the display and the various patterns create a work of art. United by color and style, these aqua jars set on a vintage shelf have a simple and cohesive feel (right). From heirlooms to new finds, china remains a favorite to include in home decor. Here, a radial display of purple Wedgwood transferware brings vibrant energy to a wall (below left). A glass-fronted cabinet keeps blue-and-white dishes safe but visible and allows them to become a strong focal point in a small recessed area (below right).

LIGHTING & ACCESSORIES

Though the primary function of light fixtures is to illuminate rooms, many of them also have decorative qualities that are equally significant. Stylish lighting makes an aesthetic statement that enhances the beauty of a home and reveals your personal style. Look out for designs that will add visual interest and help you to create a mood, and remember that placement is key to achieving the desired effect. Ambient lighting from chandeliers, pendants and wall sconces will cast a general glow, whereas smaller lamps and task lights provide focused illumination where needed. Accessories also play a consequential role in decor. They are the indispensable finishing touches that help a space come alive, shape the vibe and enrich the overall design of a home. They are the final layer that makes an interior feel complete.

FUNCTIONAL BEAUTY

Lampshades offer many options in terms of shapes, materials, colors and proportions. Rather than outshine this crystal chandelier, small lacy shades in the palest blue hue further enhance its graceful lines and classic beauty (opposite). A grouping of items linked by origin, theme, texture and tone ties in harmoniously with a home's coastal location (above left). By introducing color, vibrancy and texture, accent pillows are one of those essential accessories that go beyond just providing comfort (above center). They offer a wealth of style choices from the casual to the luxurious, with the benefit of changing the look to match the season. When embellished with bobeches (used to catch drips of candle wax), beads and pendants of similar color and material, a chandelier is much more than a light fixture. It becomes a unique accessory with a jewel-like quality (above right).

PEACEFUL PRESENCE

Successfully setting up a beautiful table begins with a curated color palette and varied textures from linens, dinnerware, glassware and silverware (above). When the essentials are in place, then it is time to layer in decorative accents such as a centerpiece composed of flowers, candles and a small figurine that contribute to the palette and theme of the tablescape. Scale and materials are also factors that need to be considered. In this instance, pale-blue glass beads are the discreet finishing touches for a dainty Parisian wall sconce, while a sleek ebony vintage bar cart gets a colorful boost from shapely aqua seltzer bottles (above right and right). Artworks, small or large, communicate balance and harmony. They contribute significantly to the visual appeal and overall character of a space by endowing it with meaning and personality (opposite).

BLUE & WHITE

Many colors are compatible with blue, as the homes in this book demonstrate, but it has a special affinity with certain hues. Above all others, blue and white is a much-loved combination. The secret power of blue, aside from delivering aesthetic beauty, is how beautifully it works with white regardless of the style or location of a home. This timeless union has the ability to evoke the unfussy charm of coastal cottages and farmhouses, yet it can also impart sophistication when used in urban dwellings. Blue and white bring continuity to a neutral scheme and a fashion-forward allure to more laid-back rooms. With a spectrum encompassing such a wide variety of shades—from peaceful and serene hues inspired by sea and sky to more dramatic tones reflecting deep oceans and storm clouds—the marriage of blue and white is perennial. It is classic, timeless, tried and true.

LASTING IMPRESSION

Though they sport different patterns ranging from faded floral, wide horizontal stripes and thin vertical lines, these three little pillows are united by their blue accents (above left). Similarly, a rustic weathered metal heart and an elegant opaline footed bowl pair up charmingly thanks to the affinity of their aqua shades—even if their materials, finishes, shapes and provenance do not appear to be made for each other at first glance (above center). A simple bouquet of blue and white flowers, such as the cloud-like blooms seen here, can enhance the aesthetic of a space while promoting a serene ambience (above right). When it comes to putting together a room, the right mix of colors, styles and accessories is a recipe for success, as this sophisticated setting clearly demonstrates with its powdery blues and pristine whites (opposite).

BEST FRIENDS

Although hues of blue work effortlessly across various styles, they deliver a timeless appeal when paired with white, as represented by this coffee table's grouping of books, flowers and glassware (above left). A white kitchen takes on a calm and intimate ambience with chairs painted in a barely there blue, a fluid table runner evoking a nearby stream and flowers that bring nature indoors (left). When accessorized with the right finishing touches, the plain drawers of a closet/built-in wardrobe punctuated with turquoise glass knobs and a chandelier enhanced with pendants act like little jewels in a hallway (above). Keeping in stride with the color theme, a louvered door wears an aqua patina while the rug adds splashes of deeper blues that tie in with the bedroom's textiles.

CLASSICALLY TRAINED

White fluffy clouds dotting a blue sky illustrate the natural kinship between blue and white (right). This cottage living room extends an invitation filled with cozy charm (below). Pillows in a variety of fabrics and patterns bring soothing yet refreshing blue notes to the sofa and chair with their cotton slipcovers, against walls painted in Farrow & Ball's All White. Artworks, plants, containers and a market basket lined with a mixed pattern of checks and stripes echo the hues of the pillows, two of which are made from vintage French ticking fabric.

THE HOMES

1

Heavenly Blues

RIGHT *Griselle sourced the ornate antique trumeau mirror online. It would originally have hung on a wall between two windows and now has a place in this formal dining room. "I wonder who enjoyed that mirror and the places it's been, and how and when it arrived in this country," she muses. Azure-hued vintage bottles are displayed on a French rack on the console below.*

OPPOSITE *Though it meant having to part with the large farm table from her previous home, the unique round shape of this room makes it Griselle's favorite space. The curved lines of the cane chairs and marble table echo those of the room itself. Even the tableware and linens have a blue theme.*

Perfect Harmony

When their eldest daughter Sarah and her family bought a home in Valencia, California, Griselle and William Fiss sold theirs in Glendale and relocated to live nearby. "I felt that 30 miles away would be too far for us to go back and forth to spend time with our two grandsons," says Griselle. "Family is very important, and we have chosen to stay close to each other."

"I am drawn to a classic feminine aesthetic that incorporates comfort and exudes a quiet elegance."

THE COUPLE'S FORMER HOME sold the first day it went on the market, which created quite a dilemma for them. "I have always lived in older homes with loads of character," recalls Griselle. "But we had to find a place in a hurry and there wasn't anything for sale in this area. Then this house popped up and we grabbed it."

It wasn't easy to go from their Cape Cod-style residence to this newer property. "However, we loved the mature greenery of the area, and the style reminded us of the old-school architecture of Glendale, where we both grew up," Griselle says. "And although it was a tract home, the house offered some lovely features that didn't feel too run-of-the-mill: the courtyard, arched doorways, tall ceilings and balconies." It took some doing to make that house a home, but Griselle got to work putting her very own stamp on the spaces. "I like to name our houses," she says. "We called this one Ma Douce Maison because I wanted to include French elements."

And so the metamorphosis began. "Our vision for both exterior and interior was to create an atmosphere that is not only appealing but also welcoming. We started from the curb and headed forward!

OPPOSITE *"I love a lot of pretty things, but aim to keep the look uncluttered," Griselle notes. She calls the den her "Frenchie-girlie room." It is furnished with a Louis XV-style sofa, an antique wall panel, nesting tables and a ruffled bench. A chandelier gleams overhead and a pink rug softens underfoot.*

ABOVE *Previously used to hold a built-in wine rack, a recess adjacent to the dining room is now home to an elegant found mirror and a French pastry table. The setting offers the perfect spot for keeping dinner-party centerpieces conveniently but stylishly on hand.*

LEFT & RIGHT *Though Griselle notes that the lack of full walls and the open floor plan have made the living room difficult to pull together, it's clear she overcame what she calls her biggest challenge. From the stylish headboard repurposed to cover the fireplace to the chairs, sofa and ottoman dressed in white and the soft blue accents, the room boasts a ready-to-entertain spirit and an understated elegance. By the windows stands another marble-topped pastry table, which Griselle has refinished.*

In the courtyard we added topiaries, espaliers, dozens of roses and bedding plants, a fountain, arbors and black-and-white cabana-striped awnings. Then we kept the French vibe flowing inside and into the back garden."

Griselle, a retired educator, has long been passionate about vintage and antiques with a focus on feminine decor. She buys and sells at established shows such as the famed Rose Bowl Flea Market in Pasadena and on her Etsy shop, named Cosy Rose Cottage after her former home in Glendale. As for William, he is semiretired from working his entire life in his family's florist shop. Griselle says, "I am so happy he loves to go shopping with me and assists me when I do my pop-up shows. I am grateful he is onboard with my decorating style and is not at all threatened by the aesthetic of our home."

Side by side and room by room, the couple undertook all the cosmetic updates needed for their 3,400-square-foot home to become the jewel it is today. Out went the old faux paint finishes and the odd golden shade of the walls in favor of white eggshell paint to brighten the rooms and provide continuity between the spaces. New floors were installed and outdated built-in cabinetry removed, including the bathroom vanities.

"We started with a clean slate, and then we slowly began to add our own touches," Griselle explains. "A lot of my previous furniture didn't work, so sadly, I had to sell it and search for the right pieces." She sought out items that were not only compatible with the aesthetic she enjoys as well as working with the scale of the rooms. "I wanted an airy feel, not cluttered with excessive furnishings or accessories. This is hard because I truly love furniture and buying things," she says.

Griselle has a wonderful eye for interiors. "My mother was extremely artistic and I can barely draw a stick figure, but I am grateful that decorating comes relatively easy and is something I truly enjoy." And she has always had a special appreciation for antiques. "As a little girl, I remember my dad taking me to an auction, where he bought me a bed. I've learned over the years from talking to dealers, doing research and asking questions from others who share the same style."

OPPOSITE *Duke, aka "Dukey," the family labradoodle, doesn't mind the openness of the living room. In fact, he appreciates the finer things in life, like the pretty blue-and-white pattern of a Laura Ashley washable rug. Instead of adding an extra sofa, Griselle chose to incorporate an antique French daybed outfitted with a cushy mattress and blue-and-white pillows that tie in with the main space.*

ABOVE *Griselle prizes this vintage desk not only for its versatility but also for its shapely style. "I have moved it from room to room, and it always plays a useful role." Paired with an equally charming chair, delicate vintage ceramics and a shapely lamp, it is at home here in the living room.*

ABOVE & LEFT *The kitchen received a major facelift. After eliminating orange glazed cabinets, a heavy iron pot rack and brown countertops, the couple installed custom cabinetry, quartz counters and a trio of chandeliers. They chose an antique table with its original blue chippy finish and French-style balloon chairs. Fresh flowers and ruffled seat pads add tender hints of pink. Vintage glass jars and serving pieces unite form with function.*

OPPOSITE *Griselle loves all kinds of collections. "To say I have a lot is an understatement," she laughs. "Even though I have pared down my possessions, I still have many that I have had fun acquiring and enjoy to this day," she explains. "Dishes, vintage and new, are in that group because I have girlfriends over frequently –I enjoy setting a pretty table so they feel special."*

WATKINS
CINNAMON

LEFT *The dainty dressing table and chair were antique finds. It is a perfect spot for Griselle to show off pieces of her collection of vintage bottles acquired from eBay and the Long Beach and Rose Bowl antiques markets. The white ironstone pitcher/jug (from yet another collection) stands atop a footed silver tray.*

BELOW *The remodeled bathroom was the latest of the many improvements undertaken by the couple. "We purchased the bathtub and the vanities three years prior to the final makeover," says Griselle, who chose two shades of marble tiles for the diagonal checkered floor. The mirror, one of a pair, was found online.*

RIGHT *In the master bedroom, Griselle's pale palette includes hints of blue and textural elements. The bed, from Eloquence, is layered with luxurious linens, including petticoat-style shams from Rachel Ashwell Shabby Chic and a floral comforter/duvet from Cabbages & Roses.*

As for a palette, Griselle favors the softness of whites and pastels. "Integrating varied hues of white with different textures has opened up the spaces and given me a feeling of peace," she says. "I can layer in the gentle, feminine shades I love, such as demure blush pink." Blue also has a special place in her home. "The softer blues bring a sense of tranquility to our rooms, and the deeper shades remind me of the ocean, where I dream of living someday."

Griselle is always ready to share her love of decorating with all, but what could be a better way than to guide the couple's youngest daughter Alyssa, who recently got engaged and just purchased a home nearby. "I can't wait to help her," says Griselle with love.

ABOVE *When Griselle found these vintage lounge chairs at an estate sale, their frames were green. Undeterred, she quickly grabbed brush and paint and, voila! To make them fit with her feminine palette, she had the cushions reupholstered with outdoor fabric in the palest shade of pink.*

LEFT *Nothing says summer like a pretty white straw hat with a wide brim. Faithful to her love of blue, Griselle has dressed it up with a striped ribbon in her favorite hue and a fragrant blossom fresh from the garden.*

OPPOSITE *This curvaceous daybed with intricate iron scrollwork came with the couple when they moved from their former home. "It was black originally, but I repainted it white," Griselle says. "It's a wonderful place to rest under the filtered light, especially with the added comfort of antique shams and squishy pillows." The bench, also painted by Griselle in powdery blue, acts as a convenient table.*

RIGHT *Rescued from an 1890s tool factory, this sizable well-preserved filing cabinet still wears its original blue paint. "I love that all the drawers are hand-labeled," Nancy says.*

OPPOSITE *Wood plank floors, matchstick shades/blinds and an iron chandelier give the dining area some weight and keep the ocean-hued space from feeling too frothy. Nancy found the chairs at a resale shop and painted them white. The vintage fireplace mantel features an Eastlake-style trim carved in low relief. The geometric tablecloth injects a modern note.*

Cottage Charm

It's never polite to rush your elders—a bit of wisdom that applies well to old houses. That's why Nancy and Rick Chace took a few years to get to know the Victorian-era cottage they bought in the historic downtown district of Bristol, Rhode Island. Just a stone's throw from the harbor, the home is nestled among shops and restaurants. "It's a wonderfully walkable waterfront community," Nancy says. "A quintessential New England town, first settled in 1680."

"I love this house because it's like a snapshot of us through time."

THE HOME ITSELF was built in 1896 and has undergone many changes over the decades. Under the Chace family's stewardship, it underwent a major refurbishment. The couple realized that while they loved their home's historical roots, they wanted brighter interiors and an updated floor plan that would work for a family with two young children. "We lived in the house six or seven years before really getting a handle on how to modify the floor plan," Nancy says, pointing out that the historic neighborhood protects the appearance of the external architecture but allows homeowners greater freedom to design the interiors. "We didn't want to extend the existing footprint of the home for budget reasons, but we had a vision of a more open floor plan, especially for the rear portion with access to the backyard," she says.

Armed with plenty of advice from architects and designers, they gutted a warren of small rooms at the back of the house to create a roomier kitchen that opens to a mudroom by the back door, and a spacious family bathroom. Other rooms have flourished under Nancy's uncanny knack for combining old furnishings with new, punctuating the decor with a smattering of industrial elements.

OPPOSITE *Nancy was overjoyed when a trip to the Brimfield Antique Flea Markets in Massachusetts yielded this hutch/dresser. "It was already dressed in white and turned out to fit perfectly between the dining-room windows." Now it cradles a medley of sturdy and inexpensive dishes, mason jars, pitchers/jugs and bowls, all in shades of peacock blue, which are regularly put to use for dinner parties.*

ABOVE *Though this mirror is new, its arched shape and simple panels confer a vintage charm that provides a pleasing counterpoint to the straight lines of the fireplace. Despite their different origins and styles, they have proved to be a match made in heaven.*

ABOVE *Just off the kitchen, the new mudroom at the back of the home serves as a family entrance. "It is so much more convenient than using the front door on an everyday basis," says Nancy. Each Chace has his or her own section, with hooks and baskets to keep seasonal gear organized.*

ABOVE RIGHT *The formerly cramped kitchen is now a roomy space featuring Shaker-style cabinets, honed granite countertops, a white subway-tile backsplash and pops of mid-century color. As with the other rooms, the different eras and styles give the space a unique charm.*

OPPOSITE *Most family meals happen around the kitchen built-in banquette. The bench seat lifts to store oversize lobster pots and other large kitchenware. The vintage sign was a fortuitous find. "Ever since we got it, nearly every family photo has been taken around that sign," Nancy says.*

She finished by enveloping everything with hues that shift from blue to green with the sunlight. "Each room and each piece received a special treatment—a wash of paint, smart slipcovers or a jaunty tablecloth—to bring it into the fold."

Speaking of the bedroom's dreamy glow, Nancy notes that though the blues and greens don't exactly match each other, they work happily together. "For me, they are soothing because they harmonize and stir up visions of the coastline," she explains. The color was the starting point and sparked every other purchase: a vintage table as nightstand/bedside table, a flea-market chair and bed linen both new and old.

CHACES
SHACK

MAP OF
LITTLE COMPTON
BRISTOL
TIVERTON
COMFORTABLE COUNTRY
CREATING A
BEAUTIFUL HOME
ALEXANDRA
STODDARD
Pretty Pastel Style
Selina Lake

"I love mixing past and current items because it makes the interiors more personal," she explains. "The rooms don't look like we made one trip to the home store."

Over the years, Nancy had discovered the transformative powers of chalk paint. "I gravitate toward watery tones," she says, "not beachy hues but softer blues, greens and bluish greens that remind me of watercolor paintings. They are so pretty and calming. Then it's just fun to drop in a pop of bright blue or even a touch of red."

The palette is the perfect backdrop for the finds she brings home. "I have a special attachment to Americana, painted furniture and vintage items," she says. The dining room notably gathers elements across eras for a design that transcends time. Together, the union of 1960s chairs, a vintage farmhouse table, a Victorian mantel and a new arched mirror is a perfect microcosm of the things she loves.

Nancy sees cottages as time capsules where people add their own touches to furnishings before passing them on to successive generations. "Our home is a witness of sorts," she says. "The belongings and collections take on a unique personality. I wanted it to have meaning, with layer upon layer from past generations and ours. I love this house because it's like a snapshot of us through time."

LEFT *The living room marries coastal and historic styles in a cozy and colorful way. A gift from his father, maps from 1895 depict three Rhode Island towns and places where Rick grew up. Nancy framed them to serve as artworks and used the greens and blues from the rivers and streams for inspiration.*

LEFT & BELOW LEFT *Once walled off, the stairwell has been opened up to the main living space. To echo the warm floors, Nancy had the railing and newels stained rather than painted, but finished the stair treads to match the blue of the wall. Shells and driftwood fragments nod to the coastal location.*

BELOW *A beachy seafoam hue sets the tone in the downstairs bathroom. A half-wall allows the sunshine to stream into the tub enclosure. The basket, striped mat and seashells add charm, color and local flavor alongside period-style floor tiles and light fixtures.*

The wall color dictated the palette of the master bedroom, where the theme of mixing old and new continues. A vintage side table and a Windsor chair have been renewed with blue chalk paint. The bedspread, pillows, accessories and seascape artwork keep the color scheme flowing, while the wood floors and headboard have a grounding effect.

RIGHT *Perched way up on a hill with an uninterrupted view of the Pacific Ocean, the small cottage miraculously survived the Malibu fires.*

OPPOSITE *This custom sofa was designed by Dawnea to fit the space and offer versatile seating options. She chose white denim with a loose fit for a relaxed yet stylish look. She describes the throw as giving "a wee kiss of blue." An old baker's table with an aged nickel surface was cut down to coffee-table height. A faux sheepskin adds comfort underfoot.*

Turning the Tide

One would surmise that living through three of the most devastating fires in Los Angeles, California would be more than enough to dissuade even the most courageous from returning to the areas that were left in ruins. But that wasn't the case for Dawnea Adams. The native Angeleno was determined to come back after the latest tragedy unfolded in January 2025. The blaze had destroyed more than 5,000 homes in Malibu, including Dawnea's, but she still felt a strong connection to the place.

With its ethereal aesthetic and calming palette, the little home exudes a sense of place. Each of the thoughtfully furnished spaces reflects Dawnea's love of a serene environment. A vintage table and cane chairs painted the palest shade of blue visually connect the kitchen and living area without interrupting the flow from one to the other.

> *"I wanted a dreamy, safe, serene space that would wrap me in peace, calm and beauty."*

"MANY YEARS AGO, when I was living in the San Fernando Valley, I was a struggling mom working three jobs to support myself," she recalls. "I had dreams of living on the ocean. Malibu was my Holy Grail—I was literally called to live there." Dawnea answered that call and has been living in Malibu for the past 43 years. "That's why, even after all the trauma and crisis, I couldn't leave," she explains.

For most people, Dawnea's background and skills are not what one might expect. She has a deep love for her Irish roots. "Both my parents' ancestors came from Ireland," she explains. "I inherited my intuitive and telepathic abilities from them, but it's my mother bloodline that runs stronger in me. I am truly a bloodline witch, gifted in every way one can be in the paranormal world."

For many years, Dawnea had been privately counseling her clients in Malibu and beyond. Though she preferred anonymity, an unexpected opportunity made her a public figure. "I was in the broom closet, so to speak, when the actress Sandra Bullock called me to consult on her film *Practical Magic*." The word got out and to this day Dawnea is known affectionately as "The Witch of Malibu."

LEFT *In Dawnea's hands, items often find a new purpose –here, a linen scarf plays the role of table runner. Be it a pretty bunch of delphiniums or a single peony, flowers are also instrumental in setting the soft and peaceful feminine ambience.*

RIGHT *The pewter-hued patina and the nailheads bordering the weathered top of the coffee table make a rustic, textural contrast to the soft silky petals of the garden roses. A glass candleholder adds a luminous note.*

OPPOSITE *The French armoire was the first piece Dawnea bought for the cottage. She added mirrors to the doors to visually enlarge the space. They reflect the gilded chandelier and the sheer batiste drapes that she calls 'the ball gowns of the home.'"*

Despite her fame, Dawnea is very private. "Allowing people into my home is huge for me," she says. "But then again, I realize that design is magic. When I walk into a space, it literally speaks to me. I call it 'intuitive design.'"

While she was evacuated during the latest fires, she stayed in a hotel. Once they were under control, she began searching for a new place in Malibu, all along manifesting the perfect home to appear. And within 24 hours she connected with the owner of this little cottage, on a street where Dawnea had lived for more than 25 years. "Imagine my surprise when I drove down the street and turned onto the driveway leading up to the tiny house on the hill. It was a full circle moment for me. The view of the ocean was stunning, and I knew I was home."

The 400-square-foot cottage was furnished with all brown pieces, including the kitchen cabinets. However, the floors were light, the appliances white and everything had been maintained and cared for. "The place was immaculate," Dawnea recalls. "I could see it as a jewel box painted in a high-gloss Chantilly Lace by Benjamin Moore so that the crystal-clear light streaming through the windows would bounce off the walls and ceiling. The white sofa, chandeliers and everything else you see now was the vision I had for the cottage at first glance."

Dawnea moved out of the hotel with nothing but a ladder and an inflatable bed. "I lived like that for six weeks and didn't care," she says. "I was just so grateful to be in Malibu again. The house spoke to me after all I had been through. I wanted a dreamy, safe, serene space that would wrap me in peace, calm and beauty."

Ever creative, Dawnea used an old iron footboard to make the standout headboard for her bedroom. The airy, graceful design of the scrolls and the feminine florals of the bed linen evoke notions of romance. Keeping pace with the charming decor, an antique cabinet has been repurposed as a nightstand/bedside table.

RIGHT *Though she would have liked to update the bathroom, Dawnea made the most of the existing features, which were in good condition. Instead, she has personalized the room with some of her trademark pieces: a brass and crystal chandelier, a hand-painted Italian wall cabinet and towels with a hint of blue.*

And Dawnea was quick to put her magical touch in motion. "I knew it had to have that faded French beauty and I thank my dear friend of many years Mark Wollman for his help finding the perfect furniture."

There was also a little garden to create, so Dawnea called on Jorge DeLuna, who had been her gardener for over 20 years, to bring her vision to life. In no time, white iceberg roses and French lavender were planted and blooming at the feet of the only thing that didn't burn in the fires: a statue of the ancient Greek goddess Nike, symbol of victory and motivation—just like Dawnea herself. How very fitting!

2

True Blues

OPPOSITE *Whitewashed ceiling beams echo the naturally weathered finish of a dresser/chest of drawers. Deep turquoise accessories enliven the neutral room. One of Erin's paintings, a vivid seascape in a wide frame made of distressed wood, reveals her connection with nature and love of contrast.* Soul, *her first large-scale horse portrait, is on permanent display. A few well-chosen architectural and industrial elements carry on the rustic theme.*

LEFT *On the fireplace mantel, Erin displays a favorite dynamic juxtaposition of dark and light with dove-white ceramic birds nesting atop a collection of vintage cobalt bottles.*

Painter's Palette

Located within commuting distance of Nashville, the town of Franklin, Tennessee boasts a historic Main Street with locally owned shops and restaurants, an antiques district and a friendly community. More than 30 years ago, artist Erin Anderson and her husband Dan fell in love with the picturesque setting and made it their home.

With its white and pale aqua palette and mix of new and old furnishings, the family room has a nostalgic cottage aesthetic. A trunk repurposed as a coffee table brings a gentle patina. Canvases painted by Erin depict mason jars and a field of ethereal Queen Anne's lace/cow parsley.

"Rotating what I display makes the rooms feel fresh and new every season."

ERIN, A CALIFORNIA NATIVE, soon discovered she loved the slower pace of small-town Southern life. She appreciated knowing her neighbors and raising her children in a home surrounded by farmland. After moving twice within the Franklin area, the couple bought a 1970s two-story home. The place looked slightly dated, but Erin relished the opportunity to create something new and soon put her heart, skills and enthusiasm to work.

She began by removing a wall between the living room and the kitchen, whitewashing the home's dark wood beams and painting the original paneling. Erin's secret weapon for dull, dark or tired-looking surfaces is paint with a matte, chalky finish. With budget in mind and her artistic background on her side, she proceeded to make her own concoction. "It's a simple, easy and economical solution," she explains. "You just need to start with one cup of latex house paint and add plaster of Paris by the spoonful and stir until the paint has a thick consistency with no lumps." She used this method to refinish, lighten and add texture and depth to the walls, the kitchen cabinets and a dark-gold fireplace.

Erin furnished her home with mainly rustic and flea-market pieces, few of which have escaped her trademark finishes.

ABOVE *Simplicity is always fresh and appealing, as the kitchen proves. The all-white scheme gets just the right lift with a selection of rustic and vintage accessories in Erin's signature colors: blue enamel coffee pots, an aqua colander and a green-painted stool. The old glass-fronted hutch/dresser keeps tableware easily accessible. "White dishes mix nicely with any color palette," Erin notes.*

OPPOSITE *The portrait of a horse from a nearby farm is part of a thoughtfully composed large-scale tableau that includes prized enamelware, canning jars and painted river rocks. "One day, I was going through my collection of handmade lace panels and placed one over one of the rocks," she recalls. "I was captivated by the juxtaposition of the white filigree against the blue-gray stone, and that sparked the idea of painting on rocks. You never know where inspiration might come from!"*

Case in point, in the kitchen's eating area, a weathered hand-me-down table and a wide bench have been renewed with her chalk paint formula. And in the family room, an old fence panel has found a new life as an accent wall, painted a light aqua but distressed to show character.

The overall palette of the home welcomes many variations of blue—from gradient shades of lapis to the ever-changing hue of azure waves, the green undertone of aquamarine and many more. These infinite mutations of blue rev up the white and gray backdrop and neutral furnishings.

Next, Erin turned to her artist's skills to create artworks inspired by nature and the subtleties of light and atmosphere. Early on, her kindergarten teacher was the first to peg her as an artist, and she's been creating beauty in many mediums ever since. "I've always been involved in art—I can't help that," she jokes. However, it wasn't until she had raised her children that Erin decided to teach herself to paint and soon began producing works inspired by her love of animals and the natural world. Her work explores the contrasts between light and dark, neutrals and bright colors, especially the extensive choices presented by a palette of blues.

Today, altered objects, treasured artworks and natural elements take center stage throughout the house. Though these decorative components are refreshed seasonally, and sometimes on a whim, some of Erin's first large pieces remain on permanent display.

Her early canvases featured animals, landscapes and coastal scenes. "I took dozens of photographs of possible subjects," says Erin.

ABOVE *In Erin's decorating ethos, textures and colors both play a big role, as witnessed in the eating area. The weathered teak garden chairs and the irregular fibers of the jute rug present a visually appealing contrast to the smoothness of the refinished table and bench. In contrast with the straight lines of the furniture, Erin has added tactile layers, including hydrangeas set in glass jars in a wire milk crate as a unique centerpiece.*

She started to post her work on social media and began selling her paintings around Franklin and at local fairs. "I have been an artist all my life," she explains. "I have dabbled in photography, garden design and jewelry making, so painting the world around me was an easy next step." And so was the transition to interiors.

What began with small paintings of mason jars kicked off a series of works featuring everyday objects that in turn led Erin to incorporate them in her decorating scheme. "I am a collector of many things, but now I can justify the items I bring home as models for paintings," she adds. "When I finish a series, I use my castoffs as decorative elements around the house."

But there are certain subjects that never stop fascinating her. The Andersons' home looks out over a pasture, which helped lead her to farm animals as subjects for her art. "I am inspired by the horses, cows and sheep that live around here," she says. "I can't get enough of those sweet faces."

Erin's home is a revolving gallery of her decorative work. "Rotating what I display makes the rooms feel fresh and new every season," she says. Since the house is a blank canvas for her art, she finds it simple to swap deeper colors for summery shades of seaglass when the time comes. "I get a thrill moving things around and redecorating," she concludes. "It's a great way to express my creative impulses."

PAGE 81 *Removing a wall between the kitchen and the living room has created a light and airy space for the family to gather. A bay window opens to the garden and blurs the boundaries between indoors and out while also reconnecting the garden chairs and table with their original function.*

OPPOSITE & LEFT *The den is decorated in a fresh and cozy cottage-meets-farmhouse style. Erin pulled the look together with furniture she has repainted in white and blue. Atop the dresser/chest of drawers, a mother-of-pearl tray corrals aqua vintage glass bottles in front of one of her evocative paintings of sea and sky. The deeper blues of the throw and carpet keep the atmospheric display grounded. Handmade birds nest in a wire basket on a table by the window.*

BELOW *Pale-blue walls make the bedroom feel like a heavenly oasis. Tiny fireflies surround an inquisitive foal and its parents in* Summer Lights, *a work from Erin's* Seasons at Tinkerbell Farm *series of paintings. Its frame was once an old screen door. The headboard was made using a wood panel with cutout filigree. Inspired by spools of old wire, Erin has snipped and twisted it into words.*

OPPOSITE *This original brick wall was one of the architectural features that Laurie fell for. "I loved the way it made the room feel—it grounds the space and gives it character," she says. "And I knew it would look great in every season." White denim slipcovers and vintage furnishings offer a soft contrast to the textural bricks and planks, while blue-painted shutters frame the window.*

LEFT *A painted metal heart, a vintage mirror and a nightstand/bedside table-turned-bookcase show Laurie's knack for mixing rustic and refined and for ingeniously pairing different shades of blue.*

Catching a Wave

For the past 31 years, Laurie Weiner has been living in her dream house, a little cottage she'd long had her eye on. She, her husband Robert and their two daughters previously lived one street over in Ventura, a quaint Southern California beach town sought after by enthusiastic surfers and windsurfers. However, when the couple bought the property, it wasn't the charming cottage it is today. As first impressions go, the small home had been neglected and nature had taken over the garden. But underneath the dismal appearance, the home ticked all the boxes for Laurie and Robert.

The sofa the couple bought when they first moved into the cottage has seen three sets of slipcovers, including the current one. "At the beginning I was into floral fabrics, but my taste evolved to prefer a less fussy look," Laurie explains. "White is so fresh and a perfect canvas for blue accents."

RIGHT *Laurie has a particular fondness for giving discarded items a new function. Set on a little old stool playing the part of a side table, she showcases a vintage glass ceiling light shade used as a bowl to display orphan chandelier crystals. "I always pick them up at flea markets and yard sales, as they also make beautiful hanging birdbaths."*

"I ALWAYS THOUGHT THE COTTAGE HAD GREAT BONES," Laurie says, "though one had to be able to see past its derelict condition and the overgrown grounds." And she did. "I knew I could make it into a cozy and inviting home for my family and friends, a place they would love to visit and linger," she continues. "When I was growing up, my mama would always have coffee and cake ready when neighbors stopped by, and I thought, 'I can't wait to do that!' My home is designed to have people over and make them feel comfortable and loved."

It was only after she and Robert purchased the cottage that she found out not everyone in the area saw it that way. "Some of the neighbors weren't very sympathetic. They would say, 'You just bought the ugliest house in the neighborhood.'" But Laurie would laugh and reply: "Just wait! We are going to make it beautiful." And with hard work and a few clever ideas, they transformed the 969-square-foot cottage into a place filled with whimsy, charm and wonder. Today, it is as open and welcoming as Laurie herself. "I am a people person," she says. "I just want everyone to feel the love in my house." And, to Laurie, the happiest look of all is white, blue and a touch of pink, with vintage treasures and chippy paintwork. "It's what cozy means to me," she says.

ABOVE *An undervalued estate-sale find, this credenza/sideboard has been reborn with a fresh coat of white. Laurie collects champagne buckets and vintage stoneware, gravitating toward white and pastel-hued pieces that unite form and function. They come in handy when she is called upon to entertain at a moment's notice–something that comes very naturally to her.*

OPPOSITE *The dining room set was originally in Robert's family home. His father applied gold-leaf accents to the chairs and did the needlepoint on their seats. An oversized mirror propped against the wall dramatically opens up the small space while adding light and depth.*

PAGE 90 *When she saw this table and chairs for sale at a vintage fair, Laurie traded one of the pieces she was selling for the set. "It was the perfect size for our small kitchen, and I loved the simplicity of the design," she says. "This part of the room overlooks the garden and is a lovely spot for breakfast."*

> *"If you like a style, just go with it. What you love will always make your home feel right."*

Raised in California, Laurie has long had a fondness for furniture and objects that display the gentle faded elegance of their past lives. "I have always decorated with pieces I truly love," she notes. "I became familiar with vintage and antiques about 20 years ago when I hosted my first flea market in my backyard. To this day, I love to learn the stories behind the pieces I collect." And Laurie is quite the collector—she has a penchant for china and glassware, with a focus on blue and pink patterns and finishes.

"I would say my favorite style falls into the shabby category," she says. "There is something so inviting about charmingly worn pieces, heaps of squishy pillows, worry-free slipcovered furniture, authentic vintage pieces and anything repurposed and reloved." So it's no wonder that her living room is both sturdy and delicate: overstuffed upholstery wears white denim slipcovers, wood furnishings sport softly weathered paint finishes and backdrops are painted a creamy white.

Laurie shops flea markets and estate sales for bargains, including ironstone and dinnerware from the 1930s and 40s, and confesses to being obsessed with bowls. For instance, she recalls the time that she and her friend Ann went to the 127 Yard Sale—the longest in the world, spanning six states and 690 miles from Michigan to Alabama. "I bought so many bowls, she thought I was secretly planning to open a salad-bar restaurant!"

Anything Laurie no longer wishes to keep for her own home, she sells at an annual yard sale she organizes with friends or sets up a booth at a local flea market.

"It keeps things fresh," she says. "If you like a specific style, just go with it. What you really love will always make your home feel right." Living by this philosophy has allowed her to embrace her preferred color palette. "I've always adored blues and pale pink. When I see it on chippy cottage pieces, I just can't even sleep."

Laurie is quick to point out she has never been attracted to shiny new things. "I like timeworn pieces that have seen a lot of love," she says. "I don't sew or paint or even cook, but I know how to shop flea markets. My friends aren't sure how I get away with it."

There is only one downside to Laurie's dream house: her husband, surfer and founder of the famous Roberts Surfboards, takes a bit of flak. "When he has people over, they often say, 'I didn't know you live in a Hansel and Gretel house!'" Laurie explains with a laugh. However, aside from giving Robert a bit of a hard time, they all love the cozy cottage Laurie created. "All our friends do—otherwise they wouldn't be our friends."

ABOVE LEFT & ABOVE *"Don't be afraid to use things you collect and don't save them for only special occasions—every day is a gift!" Laurie advises. She lives by those words, using her pretty collections of dishes daily. The kitchen credenza/sideboard shows the passage of time with peeling blue-and-white paint, a perfect match for a pitcher/jug of flowers.*

PARIS

LEFT *The bedroom gets its serene atmosphere from a palette of silvery blue and pristine white. Though simply furnished, it offers all the creature comforts. A shapely console is a handsome stand-in for the standard nightstand/bedside table–it also serves as a filing cabinet. Always thoughtful, Laurie honors her mom's memory by making one of her favorite dresses part of the decor. "She always wore it in spring."*

ABOVE *In the bathroom, Laurie introduces subtle touches of pink, her other favorite color. "This sweet pastel hue mixes nicely with gray-blues," she says, pointing to the mirror and the hamper (a former sewing basket), as well as the diminutive cabinet on the counter and the old wooden stool.*

PLANET EARTH
OVERVIEW

OPPOSITE *Linda and Neal brought these two chairs (newly reupholstered) and antique table with them from their former home. Woven baskets bring an organic touch and make a relaxed counterpoint to the formal setting. The modern floor lamp and sleek coffee table are among the touches of contemporary style to complement the more traditional elements throughout the home.*

LEFT *In the hallway facing the living room, a Windsor armchair is tucked in between an antique pine trunk and a vintage hutch/dresser. This style of chair with its continuous arm design originated in England in the 1700s.*

Coast to Coast

Even a well-known axiom such as "you can't take it with you" isn't always accurate, as former New Yorkers Linda and Neal Vitale can attest. When the couple moved to Southern California, they brought along a number of the furnishings they love and have owned for years. These priceless pieces evoke memories of their summers in Cape Cod, which is known for its quintessential New England homes.

"Luckily, many of the pieces we bought years ago have withstood the test of time."

THE ARCHITECTURE AND INTERIORS of Cape Cod reflect the influence of coastal living, as well as the region's colonial heritage and the locals' love for nature, with an emphasis on functionality, comfort and simplicity. Over the years, the nearby island of Nantucket yielded a treasure trove of antiques and collections from auctions and tag sales, including a vintage dining-room table that once belonged in a French bakery, Shaker-style woven chairs, beautifully crafted furniture made in Maine, unique artworks and an extensive collection of spongeware pottery dating from the 1800s to the early 1900s. It is a charming aesthetic that Linda and Neal wanted to adapt in their new home, far away from their beloved East Coast.

Among the features that attracted the couple to this new-build home in a well-established area of Los Angeles were the spacious dimensions of the rooms: the ample kitchen with its modern farmhouse concept and the master bedroom with its cozy sitting area and large en-suite bathroom. The versatility, character and timeless appeal of three fireplaces and the shiplap walls reminded them of their former life in New England, while the built-in bookcases offered a perfect showcase for Linda's collections.

RIGHT *The living room welcomes with its crisp blue-and-white palette. A pair of ottomans provides additional seating. Shiplap and wood paneling impart a relax mood, with contemporary art, pendant lights and a new rug injecting a touch of modernity into the otherwise classic furnishings. From decorative items to upholstery, Linda's fondness for blue is evident.*

PLANET EARTH
OVERVIEW

BELOW *The space adjacent to the dining room was originally meant to be a wine room. However, it wasn't temperature-controlled, so Linda and Neal transformed it into a handsome bar. It is cleverly outfitted with built-in storage for pitchers/jugs and glassware and shelves for artwork and bottles. Glass doors give the room its own distinct identity.*

RIGHT *A dog portrait by one of Linda's favorite artists, William Wegman, famous for his photographs of Weimaraner dogs, stands guard above a stack of little wooden trunks.*

The Vitales' vision was to create an inviting, comfortable and relaxed home, with a nod to the traditional elements they love but in a fresh way and modern way. With their classic lines, simple shapes and subtle textures, many of the pieces they owned already had the right vibe, but they needed a little help to pull it together.

So, they turned to their longtime friend designer Janet Lohman for guidance to incorporate these cherished items into their newfound nest. "This is the fourth house that we have worked on together," Janet says. "It reflects a pared-down, modern yet traditional approach that highlights their collections and art beautifully." She continues: "Linda and Neal have always been disciplined about the items they added to their homes. They both have a very strong visual 'voice' and have always been passionate about all their design decisions."

Janet and the Vitales worked together to give existing artworks, furniture and accessories a new lease of life. Windows were dressed in soft, lightweight fabrics for privacy. Existing rugs were repurposed and new ones added.

The dining table and Shaker-style white woven chairs were assembled by Neal from a kit many years ago and have followed the couple from house to house. "Luckily, many of the pieces we bought years ago have withstood the test of time," says Linda. The Sputnik-style chandelier casts a retro-modern glow.

The monochromatic contrast between the white cabinetry and the black hood and island lends the kitchen a sophisticated farmhouse style with graphic impact. Wooden stools add a handcrafted note. The quintet of pendant lights over the Shaker-style table has a vintage feel with a modern industrial twist.

Thoughtfully reupholstered pieces sit comfortably among the couple's much-loved possessions from prior homes. "Linda excels at the finishing details of each space," the designer explains. "The process made for a fun collaboration."

The living and dining rooms have an open floor plan, but each has its own identity clearly defined by their respective color schemes. The living room features an array of blue tones ranging from deep to light, and furniture both traditional and contemporary. Meanwhile, the dining room is a model of cozy simplicity with its neutral palette, new pendant lights and classic New England table and chairs. Warm woods and cool white accents are the common theme, creating an easy flow from one to the other.

The hallway leading to the kitchen and family room hosts prized vintage pieces. "We treated the antique furniture like sculpture, silhouetting them against the bright shiplap and paneling so they would stand out," Janet says. Although the kitchen has a farmhouse feel, it was conceived with elements that convey a contemporary sophistication, in order to blend it seamlessly with the refined aesthetic of the adjacent dining area.

When the Vitales purchased the home, the family room featured a black-painted brick wall surrounding the fireplace. Linda was in favor of repainting it, but Neal never wavered.

"He liked how the masculine contrast to the pale colors created an interesting tension and edginess," she explains. Built-in storage is the perfect stage for Linda to display some of her blue-and-white spongeware, which she has been collecting for more than 30 years.

Upstairs, the master bedroom is a serene and inviting retreat, with sleek shiplap walls and a modern upholstered bed. The decoration highlights Linda's preference for a crisp and contemporary direction, tempered by the warmth and texture of natural materials. This restful mood continues into the light and airy en-suite bathroom.

Despite the newness of their home, the Vitales have endowed it with a timeless feel. "Shiplap and paneling create a clean backdrop for the simple, classic lines of antique furniture and for showcasing collections," Linda says. Everything has found its place and, as Janet notes: "This home is a true testament to buying what you love!"

ABOVE & OPPOSITE *The family room is furnished with treasured pieces that continue to perform perfectly– to refresh the look, Linda replaced the sofa pillows and reupholstered the wood-framed chairs. The leather ottoman adds a modern touch. Of her spongeware pottery, Linda says: "I have so many, so I rotate them! Some of the items remain together but arranged in a new pattern." The painting by artist Janet Rickus is one of several displayed in the home.*

PAGE 104 *The master bedroom's aesthetic appeal stems from its clean lines, natural materials and gentle palette. The neutral tones of the upholstered bed and leather bench are warmed by the touchable softness of the powdery blue comforter/duvet and the deeper hue and texture of the cotton blanket. A woven basket and pine nightstand/bedside table provide earthy accents to harmonize with the wood-plank flooring.*

THE FOOD LAB

ABOVE *The seating area of the bedroom is another example of how classic and modern pieces can coexist harmoniously. The sofa and chair have been reupholstered and a textural rug added to soften the sleek coffee table. The black fireplace wall adds a graphic punchiness and dynamism to the subdued palette.*

RIGHT *Though the bathroom's brass fittings and hardware add a touch of luxury, it wasn't love at first sight for Linda. However, she eventually grew to appreciate them, along with the other fixtures and finishes that came with the home. The marble floor and the recessed shiplap walls around the bathtub contribute pattern and texture to the pristine space.*

BAR
OTEL
TALUMA
HOTEL ET VILLAS
THEVENIN
DANS LE PARC
LE MONT-DORE
AUVERGNE

3

Moody Blues

RIGHT *Michelle has brought together azure, seafoam, turquoise, indigo and pale-aqua tones to create a striking tableau on the dining-room table. In the art world, painting within a monochromatic palette like this is a technique known as* en camaïeu.

OPPOSITE *Weathered shutters framing the pass-through from the kitchen to the dining room bring a touch of vintage that Michelle loves. The antique chandelier lends romance to the room. Michelle has had the chairs for years, but repainted them a bold turquoise to impart a seaside note and provide a fresh contrast to the stylish table. Hand-scraped teak floors keep the space grounded.*

Something Old, Something New

Like many newlyweds, Michelle and Scott McCauley took the plunge and bought a home together. The spacious property on a lagoon in Novato, Northern California was a bit of a financial stretch for the young couple back then, 36 years ago, but they happily made do, especially when it came to decorating their new place. Slowly but surely, they manifested their dream home with vintage pieces and personal inspirations—their "something blue."

PRESS FOR
CHAMPAGNE

"Blue acts as a tonic counterpoint to both white and black—and I love how it connects the interiors with the beauty of the lagoon."

SCOTT, A BUILDING CONTRACTOR, often landed jobs redoing grand Victorian houses in San Francisco. At the time, many of his clients weren't interested in keeping or reselling the architectural elements torn from these old homes, and they simply gave him the goods. To those folks, it was trash. But for Michelle and Scott? Definitely treasure. Salvaged 100-year-old (and older) fireplace mantels, thick crown moldings/cornices, parts of shapely stair railings, handsome built-in cabinetry and more found their way into the couple's business—and eventually into their hearts. "I couldn't stand the thought of anyone throwing away these gorgeous things, like crystal doorknobs," Michelle says. "I wanted their history to live on as things that I or other people could use every day."

At first, their home decor was born of necessity, but it became a full-fledged love affair. "I know it sounds clichéd, but I truly value the beauty of salvaged pieces," says Michelle. In fact, she loves vintage so much that she ended up purchasing the dealers' collective Summer Cottage Antiques. There she sells overflow finds in the commercial historic downtown of Petaluma, a mere 30 minutes from her home.

"Structurally, we made a lot of changes to the floor plan, as the flow didn't work well for us when the children were young," Michelle recalls. "Fortunately, Scott was able to do all the necessary work himself.

OPPOSITE ABOVE LEFT & RIGHT *Touches of turquoise maintain the refreshing color flowing in the kitchen and on the open shelf overlooking the dining room.*

OPPOSITE BELOW *The bumped-out window over the kitchen sink offers a prime spot for a collection of ironstone and old glass bottles in soft, sea-washed hues. "I bring in all these aqua pieces because they make a visual connection with our location on the lagoon," Michelle explains.*

ABOVE *Scott built the kitchen island and Michelle added the brass-and-glass shelving unit, which is set on a marble slab for a French café feel. It adds height and provides extra space to display favorite jars, which she uses as bud vases to show off seasonal flowers.*

The living room exemplifies Michelle's flair for incorporating the colors and design elements that she favors. The black fireplace wall grabs attention and sets the eclectic tone and style for the sophisticated aesthetic of the space. The diverse mix of furnishings blends old and new and finds harmony across a spectrum of white, warmed by black accents and rich wood tones.

RIGHT *Michelle finds joy in giving castoffs a second chance and repurposing pieces throughout the house, including this weathered blue table, which takes pride of place in the living room. Seaglass beads have waterside appeal and highlight one of Michelle's favorite colors, Capri blue.*

We opened the wall from the kitchen so that we could watch the kids playing in the living room. We also removed the entire back wall facing the water and replaced it with sliding glass doors so that we could enjoy the view of the lagoon. Lastly, we took off all the carpeting and put in wood floors throughout."

Though she still prizes the patinas of well-worn paint and the graceful lines of vintage furnishings, Michelle's decorating style has evolved. Today, her Cape Cod-style cottage welcomes a mix of rough and refined, worn and pristine. "In the early years, our decor mostly had a cottage vibe and over time it has become more elevated," she explains.

But the things she treasures aren't just for show. Michelle makes it her mission to repurpose old things and make them useful again. When her children (Lauren, now 27, and Max, now 34) were young, she wanted a long, sturdy coffee table where they could color and craft, so she decided to create her own. She began with an 1800s iron gate, which Scott topped with glass and framed with crown molding/cornice. Chunky curved balusters for legs completed the project.

Likewise, a huge rusty white drying rack that was once used for wine bottles now displays a vast assortment of coffee cups in the kitchen, ready for everyday use. And a rustic former dry sink with a beautiful patina plays a starring role in the master bedroom.

SURF SHACK
SURF TRIBE

OPPOSITE *The master bedroom has the feel of an island retreat, especially with the gauzy curtains hanging from the wooden bed frame and the leafy tropical plant set in an antique dry sink. Crisp white bedding adds to the feeling of luxury. The vintage cabinet, chandelier, mirrors and bench introduce gentle rustic notes with a cottage vibe.*

LEFT *In the entry hallway, a little niche displays a charming arrangement of rare vintage flower frogs. Each holds an old brass stencil letter, sending a loving message to all who enter while expressing Michelle's attachment to enduring objects.*

BELOW *The unconventional union of formal and casual pieces works beautifully in this layered scheme. Here, an elegant 19th-century Louis Philippe mirror and crystal chandelier are contrasted with the more primitive dry sink. Its vivid turquoise turns up the volume in the mostly neutral bedroom.*

Each of these pieces is showcased against white walls that highlight the simple beauty of these vintage treasures and add character to the rooms.

For Michelle, white also offers her a blank canvas for color accents. In recent years, blue and black won her heart. "I don't know if it started with the color of the Tunisian gate we used to make the coffee table or with the dining-room chairs," she recalls. "But I love how the hues connect the interiors with the beauty of the lagoon."

More recently, Michelle has developed a fondness for touches of black. "They deliver a visual snap that adds sophistication, and blue acts as a tonic counterpoint to both white and black," she says. "It's funny how quite often things can come full circle," she reflects. "I actually used a lot of black accents when I met my husband and over time changed to white. I still love white, which is clean and provides a calm mood, but I also love the drama of a dark backdrop."

"I'm so happy Scott started saving these vintage elements before it was cool to rescue pieces of the past," Michelle says. "They speak for themselves and work so well with the updated rooms."

RIGHT *A mix of natural wood, ceramics and handcrafted linens in contrasting colors creates an authentic organic vignette.*

OPPOSITE *The living room is defined by the union of new, vintage and artisanal. "The home doesn't have a specific decor style," Lizzie explains. It embodies the Prices' preference for incorporating modern, antique and handcrafted pieces to create an interior that is not only current and timeless but also demonstrates a global flair. These qualities are represented here by the juxtaposition of a vintage bergère with a sculptural coffee table.*

Making a Scene

In most cases, before a renovation begins, it takes time for a designer and their clients to become acquainted. However, due to the long-established connection between Lizzie McGraw of Tumbleweed & Dandelion—a Californian design firm with clients from coast to coast—and Liza and Michael Price, this step had already been taken many years ago, when the couple discovered Lizzie's talents and tapped into her contagious energy.

The Curated Home
modern PASTORAL
Entertaining in the Country

"Modern, antique and handcrafted elements create an interior with a global flair."

"THE PRICES WERE AMONG MY FIRST CLIENTS back in 1997, when they lived in Westchester, New York," Lizzie recalls. "At that time, they were remodeling their first home, which because of their loyal patronage over the years we have dubbed 'Tumbleweed North.'" Both Michael and Liza are in the film industry and eventually needed to find a house in California, within easy commuting distance of their work. They found just the right one in Westwood Hills, an area famous for its many homes designed by iconic figures such as Paul R. Williams, Rudolph Schindler and Allen Siple.

This unique Los Angeles neighborhood has retained its historic past, architectural appeal and picturesque characteristics since it was originally developed in 1929. It is a true urban oasis, close to cultural attractions including the Hammer Museum and Geffen Playhouse, along with a profusion of art galleries, boutiques and eateries. And this 1950s three-bedroom home, tucked behind a picket fence on a tree-lined street, proved to be the answer to the couple's California dream.

Firmly rooted in its serene setting, the 2,300-square-foot home had already seen several redesigns over the years since the Prices moved in, all accomplished by Lizzie.

OPPOSITE *"We decided on a white linen sofa as a base for adding found pieces, textures and color," Lizzie says. Pillows made from vintage fabrics with varied hues and patterns bring in worldly touches, while warm wood accessories add modern-rustic vibes.*

ABOVE *This antique English pine dining table was the only piece salvaged from the home's previous decor. The chairs were chosen for their woven texture and honey tone. In lieu of artwork, a large wicker wall basket adds another tactile layer.*

Be My Guest
ARRIVING HOME
Dior New Looks
THE SKETCHBOOKS OF PICASSO
IMPRESSIONISM

Now the time had come for a complete overhaul, guided by the desire to emphasize the flow between the interior and the lush garden. The Prices were keen to bring a fresh, contemporary farmhouse twist to the decoration, which at the time was fairly traditional. "I was sure Lizzie would know exactly how to interpret my aesthetic of the moment," Liza says.

"Though the home had good bones and featured an inviting open plan, it was in need of a healthy reboot," Lizzie recalls. "It's a smaller cottage, so you can't really redo just one room. We started by doing a big edit and then updated each of the spaces. It's much easier to focus on one at a time."

There are many decisions to be made when remodeling a home from top to bottom, but Lizzie knew instinctively where to start. She set to work as the mastermind of the project: raising the ceilings, building a guesthouse addition and creating an exceptional elevated terrace outfitted with all creature comforts. The color blue appears in all its many tones and patterns, and new and vintage pieces are surrounded by lush vegetation and mature trees that seamlessly connect interior spaces with the outdoors. "The devil really is in the detail," says Lizzie, who is quick to praise the contractor who achieved the structural changes. "Kelin Castro of American Valley Builders Co. was a very collaborative leader, and the key to our success."

As for the new decor, the idea was to create a layered interior, not only from the point of view of soft furnishings but also with repurposed pieces. Lizzie describes her vision of "a spacious and uplifting contemporary home with vintage undertones, organic materials and flourishes of blues." Designed with comfort and conviviality in mind, the living room exemplifies this concept thanks to the winning combination of generous seating, statement lighting and curated furnishings.

LEFT *On the side of the living room facing the fireplace, built-in shelving holds more than just books. Artworks and pottery have a multicultural presence. This is further enhanced by the contrast of a pair of French chairs upholstered in vintage fabric with a reclaimed wood stool from India. Louvered doors, painted aqua and given a distressed finish, inject just the right amount of color, while 1900s warehouse-style sconces impart an industrial touch overhead.*

The space strikes a harmonious chord between relaxed family living and more formal entertaining.

The soft neutral palette has been brought to life by subtle layers of texture—the linen-look sofa, neutral rug and assortment of patterned throw pillows in rich blues and muted browns. Lizzie has married timeless forms and styles with modern function, comfort and cohesion. "We embraced traditional designs that nod to vintage style, like the English sofa with dog-friendly rugs, and added color in nooks for warmth." Except for the dining table, all the furniture here is new to the space. "This house has a history for me as well as the Prices, who raised their daughter here," Lizzie continues. "I feel like the current decoration is what the home has wanted to be for a while.

ABOVE *Successfully styled shelves begin with selecting the right objects in a variety of shapes and sizes, with a cohesive color palette. Lizzie has combined warm tones with recurring blue accents. Complementary materials and finishes are displayed in harmonious groupings.*

RIGHT & OPPOSITE *A wooden bread bowl has an organic presence in the galley-style kitchen, which is big on charm and functionality. Lizzie refinished the island to give it a weathered patina. It now serves various purposes as a breakfast spot, an additional prep station and a staging area for dinner parties. The back wall was transformed using chalkboard paint and is used for grocery lists, reminders and other messages. The Turkish runner and farmhouse sink convey a sense of vintage flair.*

BREAD

It is a little bit French and a lot Californian. It's a livable style—everything has a place and there isn't too much of anything."

When asked what the best part of working with the couple was, Lizzie says at once, "A design meeting with Liza and Michael includes wine and snacks! Over the years, we have built much more than a designer/client relationship—we have become lifelong friends. We have even been featured in magazines and now in a book together. How fun is that? But seriously, the best part is that Liza and Michael have given me a great gift in allowing me to shepherd their design journey."

ABOVE *Sustainable vintage Douglas fir boards bring a richness to the bedroom, which is further enhanced by nightstands/bedside tables in natural wicker with matching lampshades. The colorful Indian bedcover enlivens the classic stripes of the upholstered bed and ottoman. By the window is a contemporary bouclé loveseat. The eclectic mix of fabrics, colors, patterns and materials has a wonderfully cohesive effect.*

RIGHT *The right accessories can give any room a unique flavor. Set on a simple rustic stool, the timeless silhouette of a vintage French enamel pitcher/jug filled with greenery and blooms contributes to the country charm of the guesthouse bedroom.*

The guesthouse bedroom radiates a bucolic atmosphere thanks to its cheerful palette and inviting textures. The curtains' pinkish-red pattern of blooming roses on creamy linen stirs up romantic notions, while blue-and-white bed linen offers touchable textiles. A simple table and rustic bench add to the laid-back comfort of this delightful retreat.

ABOVE *Vintage French wine bottles are grouped together with terra-cotta and ceramic pots offering fragrant lavender and rosemary, graceful delphiniums and vibrant blue thistles in this tabletop display. It captures the senses with its aromatic qualities and the beauty of its still-life composition, while retaining the look of a simple, spontaneous design with an unmistakably earthy aesthetic.*

RIGHT *The terrace is a perfect example of how numerous shades of blue–along with a diverse selection of materials, textures, finishes, styles and origins–can coexist and unify a space. The sitting area easily assimilates modern chairs and a sofa, a vintage trunk and a Chinese porcelain stool. At the far end, new chairs flank a bar built from old wood and topped with marble. In the abundance of the lush and leafy surroundings, the two areas feel organically connected to one another.*

OPPOSITE *The kitchen renovation gave Nikki a chance to come up with just the right finishes and palette to complement the rest of the house. White cabinetry was a must, as was the inclusion of open shelves where she could display blue glassware and showcase shells and other seaside elements. "I wanted the kitchen to be streamlined, functional, simple and orderly," she explains. "Everything has a place."*

LEFT *The exterior is painted a soft green with a contrasting white trim, picket fence and arbor/pergola to reflect the local foliage, the sky and the white sandy beach.*

Go with the Flow

It is said that beauty is in the eyes of the beholder, and this holds true where Nikki and Jeff LaBelle's home is concerned. When they first saw their island cottage, it was outdated and in need of work. However, the unspoiled beauty of the remote Florida location surrounded by water and close to one of the world's most beautiful beaches, only 10 minutes from the mainland, proved irresistible.

"I wanted our home to be a place where everyone was welcome."

THE COUPLE HAD AGREED that they wanted a home where their children could grow up in a quiet and safe area and enjoy the health benefits of such an environment, although Jeff wanted a place on the Bay and Nikki favored the beach. Luckily, with the Gulf of Mexico in the front and the back facing the Sarasota Bay, the cottage was the perfect compromise. Over the years, they kept improving and expanding their home. Every inch of the cottage has been completely transformed from its original 1980s style to become the dream beach house it is today.

The overall aesthetic was inspired by the coastal location and by Nikki and Jeff's laid-back, family-focused lifestyle. The work began with knocking down walls and raising the sunken family room to help the rooms connect and breathe so that all the main floor's spaces could become one large and bright open living area. The next step was to replace old broken tiles with nailed-in wide-planked wood floors. To add an aged look, Nikki encouraged her children to ride their skateboards and tricycles on the wood—an unusual way to create instant patina.

Stucco walls and popcorn ceilings gave way to white-painted tongue and groove with a touch of blue to give the home a seaside feel.

OPPOSITE *The family room is outfitted with comfortable sofas and sturdy tables that can withstand daily use. Together, the vintage chair and armoire instill the right touches of elegance to counterbalance the more casual furnishings.*

ABOVE *A long rustic wooden bench makes a perfect spot for keeping straw hats—handy for walks on the beach. Frames made from recycled wood hold favorite family photos. Striped pillows in pale hues of blue, green and sand speak of the home's surroundings.*

OPPOSITE *Nothing says "beach-house chic" like a coastal blend of aqua, turquoise and soft white. Offering a picture-perfect vista, the kitchen's cheerful breakfast nook with a built-in bench is the family's preferred spot to share their daily meals. Nikki painted the back of the new cabinets a soft sky blue to echo the nearby ocean. The chandelier's delicate bobeches and pendants have the charm of seaglass.*

ABOVE *A wall of French doors allows the view of the terrace and the Sarasota Bay beyond. It's the LaBelles' preferred area to host large dinner parties. "We have invited as many as 100 friends at a time," says Nikki. "We like to share what we have."*

ABOVE RIGHT *Nikki always looks for pots and other containers with a design, shape and color that ties in with her established palette and connects with each room. Shells, starfish and sand dollars are some of her other favorite decorating staples.*

Upstairs, a master suite was added to the existing four bedrooms. Now the Florida sunshine pours into the whole house through unadorned floor-to-ceiling windows. Nikki and Jeff not only altered the home structurally but cosmetically as well. However, that isn't all. On the outside, they built terraces and a loggia to entertain to their heart's content.

Nikki's goal was to create a spacious, relaxed, bright and stylish interior that would invite with what she describes as an "easygoing, put-up-your-feet" attitude. "With four children and three dogs," she continues, "I wanted our home to be a place where the kids could truly be comfortable and everyone was welcome." This ethos is ideal for entertaining. "In order to be a happy host, you have to be a relaxed host. It's not fun to visit a house where you feel you can't touch anything or feel at ease anywhere!" With that in mind, she had her couches slipcovered in white denim, which is surprisingly low-maintenance.

"I throw the covers in the wash every couple of weeks and they look good as new. Any stains from the dogs' wet paws or the kids' sandy feet disappear. Nothing is off-limits in this house."

To help establish the easy elegance and carefree ambience she sought, Nikki turned to her longtime friend Susie Holt and her beloved shop Posh in nearby Venice, Florida. Underscored by calming blue accents that mirror the surrounding waters, one-of-a-kind antiques and heirloom pieces with worn and chipped finishes contribute to the inviting seaside vibe of the open-plan living area.

Looking around the LaBelles' home, there are countless reminders of their family values and their beach lifestyle. Weathered furnishings ground the interiors, and walls are decorated with surfboards and reclaimed wood frames that display pictures of happy memories with Nikki and Jeff's children. Blue and aqua accessories, seashells and nautically inspired books pay further tribute to the location. Though Nikki kept the furnishings in the main living space comfortable and hard-wearing so that they would withstand daily use, she is a romantic at heart and made sure to include a few feminine touches such as crystal chandeliers and the master bedroom's pretty bed linens.

Making the most of coastal living is everything to the LaBelles. "We are water people," Nikki likes to say.

The spacious living room is bathed in natural light and offers wonderful views of the lush tropical surroundings thanks to floor-to-ceiling windows. The new couches are paired with a vintage coffee table and credenza/sideboard. Blue and aqua accents and shells of all shapes and sizes contribute to the calming ambience.

LEFT *A large bathroom is the ultimate luxury, and for Nikki it is a quiet escape where she can relax and recharge. Borrowing space by enclosing a former balcony provided room for a stand-alone tub and an additional dressing area. Marble floors add a touch of sophistication. The surrounding flora creates a verdant backdrop outside the windows to enhance the spa-like mood.*

OPPOSITE *The bedroom is all about romance, comfort and simplicity. Nikki's penchant for antiques is demonstrated by a vintage mirror constructed from a salvage frame. Its rustic finish is balanced by ruffled bed linen that stands out crisply against the seafoam walls. A small nightstand/ bedside table and a French-style chandelier with aqua pendants are the perfect finishing touches.*

"The kids are avid surfers and Jeff and I enjoy paddleboarding. He spends time harvesting crabs from the bayside and fishing for tarpons, while I collect shells and put them around the house or use them in crafts." Entertaining plays a big role, too. "We enjoy having our family and friends over for evening bonfires and fishing."

Making the most of their waterside location is everything to the LaBelles. The beauty of Nikki and Jeff's beach house comes from its informal charm and their desire to share it with all. The interior reflects their lifestyle, bringing together coastal comfort and chic elegance in perfect harmony.

4

Atmospheric Blues

OPPOSITE *Peg found the perfect place for a tall and narrow armoire that she bought 35 years ago. The ample French champagne basket, from an antiques store in San Francisco, was once used for harvesting grapes and has now been put to work again, this time to store blankets and linens. Wearing their blue-and-white sweaters, Margot and Moose the Boston Terriers are well matched to the room's palette.*

LEFT *True to her love of pieces that have retained their original finish, Peg has paired an antique French table with a vintage enamel shelf and fresh blue accents.*

Pretty Mélange

California born and raised, Peg Schrader's roots are firmly grounded in her home state. "I am originally from the San Francisco Bay Area and spent most of my life in Marin County, just north of the Golden Gate Bridge," she explains. But when she recently retired, Peg knew it was time to make a move.

The spacious living area is Peg's favorite space. "It's a long and narrow room, but it's light and bright and I love how it feels," she says. "I bought the large French chandelier for the highest point of the ceiling. It's not connected to electricity, so it truly is jewelry for the house."

RIGHT *Peg excels at composing little vignettes like this one. Vintage landscapes from France watch over a marble bistro table holding a simple grouping. It is composed of one of the antique aqua seltzer bottles from her collection, a Moroccan glass in a similar tone and a lush bouquet of fresh-from-the- garden hydrangeas in powdery blues that soften the more vibrant items.*

SEVERAL YEARS EARLIER, Peg had visited Sutter Creek, a picturesque former gold-mining town full of history. "I remembered how charming and friendly it was," she recalls. "And I liked the idea of getting away from the hustle and bustle of the city. Yet it's only a two-hour drive from the Bay Area, so I can visit my family and friends and they can visit me!"

The 1,500-square-foot Victorian cottage she ended up buying wasn't even on the market. "I heard that the owner was considering selling and I took it from there," says Peg. She went to look at the home and fell in love with the high ceilings, the porches, the wainscoting, the original windows and doors and the gardens. A deal was struck.

"The house had been much loved, and the previous owner spent years working on it," she notes. "I benefited from her improvements—she had raised the ceilings and redecorated the two bathrooms with new marble floors." However, the pink exterior was in need of new paint. "Refreshing it with several coats of white was the first thing that I had done before I moved in," Peg says. Inside the house, the next step was to repaint the living room, bedrooms and office in her preferred palette.

The former storage outbuilding didn't escape Peg's transformative vision, which began with painting the walls white and adding sheer curtains on the existing windows but keeping the original floor intact. Outfitted with a rustic farm table, mismatched chairs from her previous home, one-of-a-kind side tables and subtle blue accents, the dining shed, as Peg named it, now accommodates convivial gatherings in style.

OPPOSITE ABOVE *This buffet in the kitchen sets the aesthetic tone for the upcoming remodel of the space. "After seeing it in an antiques store, I couldn't stop thinking about it–I had to get it," Peg confesses. "The color is so layered that it shifts between blue, gray and green depending on the time of day."*

"I love the look of different blues together, from navy to cerulean."

"The wooden floors are original, but the hue was too orange for my taste. The walls were painted as well to keep everything consistent, bright and neutral," she says. "White looks good with everything—it's the perfect crisp backdrop for vintage items, natural wood pieces or those that have been painted and are a bit chippy."

As for blue, she is quick to admit that it's the color she has always gravitated toward, regardless of passing trends. "I don't care what the in-style color is," she emphasizes. "I love the look of different tones of blue together, from navy to cerulean and all the shades in between. Those reflecting the ocean and the sky just really resonate with me."

The property came with a 200-square-foot barn-style outbuilding located just a few steps from the kitchen; Peg saw its potential and transformed it into what is now known as the dining shed. "It already had these old, fabulous wood floors, beadboard ceilings and windows and was connected to the electricity. I thought it would make a perfect spot for dinner parties." Now that all the cosmetic improvements have been done, Peg says she is going to focus on the kitchen. "It needs a full remodel, but at least I have this great cupboard, which has set the tone for the space's future aesthetic."

Peg's comfortable style is a lesson in blending textures and reclaimed wood with the femininity of crystal lighting fixtures, dainty florals and varied hues of blue. Her relaxed and intuitive approach to decorating, with nothing too formal or matching, results in a pretty mélange of California casual and French charm.

RIGHT *In keeping with the rustic-chic allure of the dining shed, Peg has united mismatched French vintage silverware and transferware dishes. Glass candleholders, napkins and frilly cornflowers in individual vases underscore the recurring blue theme.*

BELOW *The bathroom had been updated with a marble floor before Peg bought the cottage. She refreshed the existing paneling using gray paint with a blue undertone and added the vintage mirror to fit with the pedestal sink and the claw-foot tub. The little wooden stool is an old shoe worker's bench. "It wears its original color–it's such a sweet little piece," Peg says.*

"I am attracted to authentic old pieces, a light and clean palette and the discreet glamour of vintage chandeliers," she says. "I don't intentionally add anything, but I tend to fall for items that are both functional and beautiful, such as baskets, throws, pillows and natural-fiber rugs."

Fortunately, both Sutter Creek and the Bay Area offer plentiful shopping options for lovers of unique goods. Among her many favorite local sources, Peg cites her friend Maria Carr of Dreamy Whites Lifestyle, located a mere five minutes away in Amador City.

Though she only moved into the cottage in September 2024, Peg has already made it hers. "I am lucky that the former owner loved gardening and had planted a wide variety of trees and shrubs," she says. "During my first spring here, it was so much fun to see what was blooming: daffodils, dogwood, wisteria, lilacs, roses, sweet peas, lavender, jasmine and many more."

Inspired by the existing landscaping, Peg has planted lots of hydrangeas, larkspur and delphiniums, and is now getting ready to tackle the lower part of the property. "I can see myself growing lettuces and herbs there, but most of all I want to establish a cutting garden—with an abundance of blue flowers, of course!"

A plain headboard is made charming when dressed in a blue floral fabric from famed British company Cabbages & Roses. In lieu of a traditional coverlet, Peg laid a vintage French mattress cover on top of the comforter/duvet. Its blue stripes are a deeper shade than those of the pillow, but they play nicely with each other and with the mirror and dainty sconces.

OPPOSITE *Though everything she has acquired over time resonates with Peg, some items have a greater significance than others and are prized more for their emotional connection than their monetary value. "The antique French daybed came from a friend, and I used to have it on the porch of my former home," she says. "And the green garden bench belonged to my grandfather, who worked as a gardener after immigrating from Italy. They are very special to me."*

ABOVE *A pillow and mattress made of vintage French ticking fabrics add comfort to a teak lounger and an Adirondack chair nestled under a shady tree. The wagon was a retirement gift from Peg's coworkers. "It works perfectly in my large yard and helps me with my gardening tasks, for example carrying plants, tools and bags of soil–and Margot and Moose love riding in it!"*

RIGHT *The moment she laid eyes on this French bistro table in an antiques shop, Peg just had to have it. "I fell in love with the color," she recalls. Set on a sheltered little porch, it offers a prime view of the garden.*

RIGHT *A tall bookcase displays an assortment of favorite aquamarine vintage objects from Amy's collection. For visual interest, she chose pieces in varied heights, shapes, sizes and hues.*

OPPOSITE *A primitive chest-turned-coffee table and a deconstructed wing chair offset the feminine style of the living room. Nesting tables were painted blue and finished with a light silver coat for an elegant touch. In her first attempt at fine art, Amy used chalk paint to create the landscape over an inexpensive rose painting. The fearless hands-on decorator also transformed the plain fireplace mantel with Efex appliqué moldings.*

Tried and True

According to decorator Amy Chalmers, this 14-year-old Colonial-style prefab is the least-likely home she could have imagined herself living in—and yet it is the one she's occupied the longest. "As a single mom, I tended to live in old houses," she says. "Each time I'd fix it up, sell it and get another one." For this dramatic change of address, she has love to thank.

CHARLES FAUDREE
RACHEL ASHWELL Couture PRAIRIE
SEGRETOvignettes

OPPOSITE & RIGHT *Amy learned her hands-on home skills from her parents. "They were always doing projects with us kids in the mix," she says. "There's really no creative concept we would shy away from." This includes the sofa's white slipcover, which she sewed 10 years ago using cotton duck cloth. The clean backdrop lets her change her look by swapping pillows and accessories. Most of the accessories are in tones of aqua, but Amy has also incorporated touches of pink for a little contrast.*

SHE WAS DATING HER NOW-HUSBAND Dave when he asked her to decorate his new place. "I decorated it for him in his style," Amy says. "Then when we finally hooked our wagons, I set about giving the new home an old-house feeling."

For this hands-on decorator and lifelong antiques lover, layering on character starts with color and collections. "Color is the biggest, and least-expensive, decorating tool available to anybody, from beginners to professionals," she says. "It has the single greatest impact. You just have to have the confidence to use it."

As a background, Amy chose her favorite aquamarine and pale celery tones. The soft, livable hues act like neutrals, mixing easily with her go-to accent colors: silvery gray, pale purple and metallic gold. Her collections add both a vintage feel and touches of freshness, especially two of her favorite obsessions: opaline glass and purple Wedgwood transferware. These pieces aren't hidden away in cupboards; they are on full display and in frequent use. "My collections aren't just there to be looked at," Amy says. "They are things we can use every day."

ABOVE *The kitchen is on the smaller side, so Amy decided to give it cottage character by painting the cabinets white. She removed cupboard doors above the stove vent/extractor fan to create an open niche for displaying collectibles and added the carved molding. Toile de Jouy curtains and a geometric rug add harmonious green notes to the mix.*

OPPOSITE *Thanks to the dining room's hushed colors, an enviable collection of purple Wedgwood dishware takes center stage against the celery hue of the hutch/dresser. "Green is the color that makes everybody play nicely together," Amy says.*

Amy finishes almost every space with her favorite and most useful decorative collection of all. "I am crazy about vintage lighting," she admits. She's been known to get into bidding wars at auctions, which is how she snagged the French basket chandelier that is now a focal point in the dining room. It's a lovely contrast to the farm table that her son instantly aged with a coat of pale blue-gray paint.

With the same goal of incorporating elegant touches, she used stamped-in moldings/cornices that she found hiding in an antiques shop and repurposed them for the windows. Vintage table and bed linens have been fashioned into curtains. "I'm allergic to just buying what you want at a store," Amy explains. "I want to figure out a way to create it or alter it. To me, the process is a big part of enjoying the end result."

Adding a few rough-hewn pieces to each room is a must for Amy in the beautiful balancing act going on in this house, all by design. "I like mixing the rustic with the finer elements," she explains, "so rooms don't become too precious or girlie. If you think your spaces are getting too fancy or museum-like, just add a few primitive pieces."

Balance is indeed struck in the master bedroom with the dark wood of a new paneled bed. It's a piece that brings harmony to the room in ways that go beyond the aesthetic. "This was a bedroom set that my husband picked out," Amy says with a laugh.

"If you think your spaces are getting too fancy or museum-like, just add a few primitive pieces."

"He begged me not to paint it, which goes against my instincts. So, I call this my husband's room that I just sleep in. But everywhere I look I see my hands or Dave's on this house. It brings a sense of pride and fulfillment."

Asked to define her style, Amy explains, "I'm drawn to the French Rococo look; I love to add things with a little curve. It makes a room more exciting. So, I'd say my style is vintage and elegant. But it has to have comfort mixed in—that's my number one rule."

LEFT *The dining room opens into the living room, so Amy created flow by shifting the soft blue color palette to an elegant silvery blue-gray. The crystal chandelier and French cane-back chairs soften the rustic farmhouse table. For added cottage charm, Amy embellished the curtains with a pom-pom trim.*

PAGE 158 *To give the relatively small master bedroom a more dramatic look, Amy arranged it on the diagonal. This is a strategic solution when a room has limited wall space for a headboard. Pretty linens in colors pulled from a favorite painted French table used as a nightstand/bedside table lighten up the stately bed frame.*

BELOW *Amy pays careful attention to details and chooses accessories to coordinate with their setting, from jewelry cradled in a mercury dish to fresh flowers selected specifically for their hues.*

ABOVE & RIGHT *Amy has created the look of an elegant dressing room in this bathroom with the right extras, including a vintage brass mirror and a pegboard strung with colorful costume jewelry. A vintage French hotel caddy and other hints of aquamarine weave her favorite color into the upstairs rooms for design continuity.*

RIGHT *On a slipcovered chair, an indigo pillow and throw add to the home's comfy vibe. Books on topics ranging from travel to home decor invite moments of reflection.*

OPPOSITE *One of Barbara's favorite finds is this vintage shelving unit, which she uses to organize a large collection of inspirational magazines. "It was originally a sorting shelf used by schoolteachers," she says. Nautical accessories such as model sailboats and coral keep the coastal environment present. Though their patterns and hues differ, the chair and the ottoman mesh harmoniously. The wood table adds warmth to the cool palette.*

Seaside Bliss

Ask Barbara and Bruce Gray and they will tell you how easy it is to love Southern California with its temperate climate, indigo waters, vibrant coastline and surfing vibes. So, when a home became available in La Jolla, the dramatic setting of the property captured the couple's attention and drew them to purchase it.

beach house style
WREATHS
1
2
3

"The blues and whites flow out to where the sun shines on the cresting waves."

THERE ARE VIEWS...and then there are Views with a capital V—and the latter is one of the most wow-worthy attributes of the Grays' home. Their 1960s ranch-style house rises above stunning Windansea Beach, capturing a breathtaking panorama of the Pacific with waves rolling onto a long arc of sandy shore. "Nearly every room here has direct water views," says Barbara. "It's a dream scenario—each day by the sea holds a beautiful surprise." She often works at her dining-room table, finding inspiration for her interior-design business simply by looking out and letting nature fuel her imagination.

When she is designing, Barbara channels that creative energy into her own home, infusing spaces with a unique combination of casual comfort and California chic. Her secret is in the mix of humble pieces with finer, more traditional designs. "I like pairing vintage and repurposed treasures with classic favorites," she says. "I wanted this home to feel comfortable. It is a large house, but it doesn't feel that way because the colors, furnishings and accents unite to create a sense of coziness and intimacy."

The classic coastal palette of blue and white is woven through every room of the house. Barbara first borrowed hues from the sapphire ocean and the azure sky.

PAGES 162–163 *A wall of windows wraps around the front of the home to capture the ocean views from its elevated position. Tidal and surf-washed hues blur the lines between indoors and out and forge a close connection with the coastal vista. Down-filled linen furnishings provide comfort to while away the hours. The weathered finish of the vintage tray and flower bucket bring the dreamy setting down to earth.*

LEFT & OPPOSITE *Pearly seashells add a refined touch to the decor. The dining table, which seats up to 14 people, doubles as Barbara's workspace during the day. The view is a constant source of inspiration. White linen-upholstered seats lighten the look of the hand-carved oak chairs. Wood floors and furniture pieces provide a warm contrast and balance the coolness of the many blues of the accessories.*

BELOW LEFT *Whichever way you turn, there is always a sprawling sight of the ocean. This armchair swivels to face the sunset and gets a long side view of the beach below during the day. For contrast and visual interest, Barbara paired a marble-and-wood antique side table with a new blue-and-white rug in a simple yet striking checkerboard pattern.*

She layered these with tones that echo the rhythms of the white-capped breakers. "From my family room, the blues and whites flow out onto the balcony to where the sun shines on the cresting waves."

Plump upholstered pieces and cushy pillows provide irresistible perches to take in the vistas, enticing family and friends to gather round. "I use a lot of slipcovered down chairs and plump pillows to instill that sense that you really want to sink in and relax," Barbara says. "Plus, they give that beachy-chic feel."

For most rooms, white walls offer a clean slate. "Then I can add any color I want," she says. "In this case, blue and white connect the interiors to the idyllic beach setting." Along with upholstered seating and ottomans, Barbara has brought in natural wood for warmth and mixes in nautical accents and other small treasures that emphasize her coastal-inspired color palette.

"There is always a new take on blue-and-white fabrics to love," Barbara says. And with her keen eye for design, she masterly incorporates soft and tactile cotton and linen textiles. Pillows and throws with rich indigo dyes enliven the custom armchairs, with aqua and turquoise accessories that recall the ever-changing hues of the sky above and the ocean below.

LEFT & OPPOSITE *Barbara brought color and texture to the master bedroom wall by using a faux paint technique on one wall to mimic the African indigo fabrics that she loves. The deep blue creates a pleasing contrast to the crisp white cotton of the upholstered headboard. The 1930s French comforter/duvet cover displays hand-stitched cutwork and needlepoint. The antique French cane settee sits on an aqua rug. Pillows fashioned from favorite fabrics and a ceramic table lamp keep the color scheme on track.*

One of her favorite, more whimsical accents is a sign that says: "Heaven's a little closer in a house by the sea." That pretty much sums up how Barbara and Bruce feel about their little slice of paradise. "After work, he and I like to meet in the living room and then have dinner on the veranda," she says. "We don't go out to eat because I love to cook, and there's no restaurant with a better view." Indeed, in the Grays' home with its sweeping oceanic vistas, every cozy chair becomes the best seat in the house.

Barbara's home reflects her personality and surroundings. As she says, "Ultimately, my style has a casual coastal feel—and that's how I see myself." Her design philosophy proves that whatever you put into your home, your home gives back to you.

RIGHT *In the bathroom of the guest bedroom suite, Barbara strayed a little from her preferred palette and played with yellow accents. However, she remained faithful to her favorite classic combination by introducing a striped blue-and-white rug.*

OPPOSITE, RIGHT & FAR RIGHT *On a balcony off the family room, a teak dining set seats eight and enjoys a view that rivals any beachside restaurant. "This is where we have breakfast, lunch and dinner," Barbara says with delight. "It's like a storybook, isn't it?" The blue rhapsody extends to every detail, from the spotted silverware caddy to the azure and aqua glassware.*

ABOVE *The blue-and-white theme continues on the poolside patio with two upholstered chairs that invite guests to relax in style. The design of the pool evokes the natural curve and movement of a wave, while the water's deep-turquoise hue echoes that of the Pacific. Stone paving harmonizes with the sandy beach below.*

SOURCES

SHOPS

Dreamy Whites
www.dreamywhitesatelier.com
IG: @dreamywhiteslifestyle
Exclusive imported French and Swedish antiques, linens and accessories.

Grenouille French Vintage
San Francisco, CA
(by appointment only)
www.grenouillefrenchvintage.com
IG: @grenouillefrenchvintage
Importing vintage treasures for the home and garden for over 25 years.

The Antique Gardener
Sutter Creek, CA
www.facebook.com/theantiquegardener
IG: @theantiquegardener
An ever-changing selection of European and American garden furniture, planters and architectural salvage.

The Vintage Nest
Fillmore, CA
IG: @thenestfillmore
Vintage and timeless finds online and in store.

The Winsome Nest
Walnut Grove, CA
www.winsomenest.com
IG: @thewinsomenest
French country antiques, farmhouse decor, handcrafted gifts and homewares from around the world.

Vignettes
San Diego, CA
www.vignettesantiques.com
IG: @vignettesdecor
Exclusive vintage home decor with an emphasis on rustic French country pieces and architectural elements.

ONLINE

ABYU Lighting
www.abyulighting.com
One-of-a-kind light fixtures made by hand with exquisite materials.

Annie Sloan
www.anniesloan.com
Annie Sloan, CBE, invented her revolutionary Chalk Paint in 1990 and is one of the world's leading authorities on paint, color and style.

Ashcroft & Tibbles
www.facebook.com/AshcroftandTibbles
IG: @ashcroftandtibbles
Sculptures, busts, staddle stones, urns, garden benches, fountains, birdbaths and so much more.

Atelier de Campagne
www.facebook.com/
AtelierdeCampagneLLC
IG: @atelierdecampagne
All things for the home and garden.

Bella Notte Linens
www.bellanottelinens.com
Linens designed for beauty and comfort, made with a passion for color and craftsmanship.

Big Daddy's Antiques
IG: @bigdaddysantiques
Significant and statement-making pieces for the home and garden.

Bountiful Home Antiques
IG: @bountifulhomeantiques
A treasure trove of European and American vintage finds.

Cabbages & Roses
www.cabbagesandroses.com
Exquisite textiles featuring deliciously faded florals and other enduring English patterns.

Crate & Barrel
www.crateandbarrel.com
With a distinct architectural aesthetic, Crate & Barrel connects the creative work of artisans and designers to people and places around the world.

Eloquence
www.eloquence.com
Refined interpretations of the finest antique furniture.

Elsie Green
www.elsiegreen.com
IG: @elsie_green
A secret source of vintage French homewares and treasures.

Euro-Linens
www.euro-linens.com
A variety of European textiles, from grain sacks to placemats.

Love Shack Fancy
www.loveshackfancy.com
Luxurious bedding, homewares and accessories.

Marina Natalia
www.marinanatalia.com
IG: @_marinanatalia
Home and garden decor from France, Belgium and the Netherlands.

Mark Wollman Antiques
IG: @markbiltvintage
Unique antiques from around the world.

Matouk
www.matouk.com
Exceptional linens, handcrafted from the world's finest materials.

Pom Pom at Home
www.pompomathome.com
Lived-in yet elegant linens since 1991.

Pottery Barn
www.potterybarn.com
Beautiful items crafted to last for the home and garden.

Rachel Ashwell Shabby Chic
www.shabbychic.com
IG: @officialshabbychic
Graceful heirloom pieces that combine all the best of modern style and classic vintage charm.

Room and Board
www.roomandboard.com
Beautiful, practical and timeless modern furniture with a focus on simplicity and functionality.

Shabby Whites
www.etsy.com/shop/Myshabbywhites
IG: @shabby_whites
Vintage French, romantic and shabby-chic items.

Shaker Workshops
www.shakerworkshops.com
Shaker furniture is the one truly original American style of furniture, with crisp lines that complement traditional and modern settings alike.

Thos. Moser
www.thosmoser.com
Simple, sustainable furniture that celebrates the natural beauty of wood and is crafted for a long, useful life.

Weston Table
www.westontable.com
IG: @westontable
An artisanal marketplace for the conscious consumer that showcases provenance, authenticity and creativity.

ANTIQUES MARKETS

Aubergine Emporium
Simi Valley, CA
IG: @auberginemporium
Vintage furniture and unique home decor.

Brimfield Antique Flea Markets
Brimfield, MA
www.brimfieldantiquefleamarket.com
One of the most attended shows in the US, thanks to its exclusive French and European antiques.

Long Beach Antique Market
Long Beach, CA
www.longbeachantiquemarket.com
A monthly event established in 1982.

Rose Bowl Flea Market
Pasadena, CA
www.rgcshows.com/rose-bowl
Known all over the world because of the uniqueness of the items for sale.

Santa Monica Antique and Vintage Market
Santa Monica, CA
www.santamonicaairport antiquemarket.com
A destination for decorators, designers and boutique owners.

The Agoura Antique Mart
Agoura Hills, CA
www.theagouraantiquemart.com
1,300-square-foot gallery-format showroom specializing in antiques, gifts and home decor.

The Santa Barbara Antique Show
Santa Barbara, CA
www.sbantiqueshow.com
IG: @sbantiqueshow
Held twice a year, this show brings the finest antiques and vintage dealers to Santa Barbara.

PICTURE CREDITS

All photography by Mark Lohman.

Key: a = above; b = below; l = left; c = center; r = right.

1 The home of Peg Schrader;

2 © Mark Lohman/The home of Nancy and Rick Chace;

3 © Mark Lohman/The home of artist Erin Anderson and her husband Dan;

4 The home of Neal and Linda Vitale in Los Angeles, California;

5 The home of Peg Schrader;

6 © Mark Lohman/The home of Amy and Dave Chalmers;

7 The home of Barbara and Bruce Gray;

8–9 © Mark Lohman/The home of artist Erin Anderson and her husband Dan;

10–11 The home of Neal and Linda Vitale in Los Angeles, California;

12 The home of Robert and Laurie Weiner in Ventura, California;

13 l The home of Griselle and William Fiss;

13 c The home of Liza and Michael Price;

13 r The home of Barbara and Bruce Gray;

14 al & ar The home of Peg Schrader;

14 bl The home of Barbara and Bruce Gray;

14 br The home of Petaluma, CA antiques store owner and designer Michelle McCauley;

15 a The home of Dawnea Adams;

15 b The home of Griselle and William Fiss;

16 l The home of Liza and Michael Price;

16 c The home of Peg Schrader;

16 r The home of Barbara and Bruce Gray;

17 © Mark Lohman/The home of artist Erin Anderson and her husband Dan;

18 © Mark Lohman/The home of Nancy and Rick Chace;

19 al The home of Liza and Michael Price;

19 ar The home of Peg Schrader;

19 b The home of Neal and Linda Vitale in Los Angeles, California;

20 The home of Liza and Michael Price;

21 l © Mark Lohman/The home of artist Erin Anderson and her husband Dan;

21 c & r The home of Petaluma, CA antiques store owner and designer Michelle McCauley;

22 a © Mark Lohman/The home of artist Erin Anderson and her husband Dan;

22 b The home of Robert and Laurie Weiner in Ventura, California;

23 al The home of Griselle and William Fiss;

23 ar The home of Liza and Michael Price;

23 bl The home of Barbara and Bruce Gray;

23 br The home of Griselle and William Fiss;

24 l The home of Petaluma, CA antiques store owner and designer Michelle McCauley;

24 c The home of Peg Schrader;

24 r © Mark Lohman/The home of artist Erin Anderson and her husband Dan;

25 The home of Petaluma, CA antiques store owner and designer Michelle McCauley;

26 The home of Neal and Linda Vitale in Los Angeles, California;

27 a The home of Griselle and William Fiss;

27 bl © Mark Lohman/The home of Amy and Dave Chalmers;

27 br & 28 The home of Griselle and William Fiss;

29 l © Mark Lohman/The home of Nikki and Jeff LaBelle;

29 c The home of Robert and Laurie Weiner in Ventura, California;

29 r © Mark Lohman/The home of Nikki and Jeff LaBelle;

30 l The home of Griselle and William Fiss;

30 ar The home of Peg Schrader;

30 br The home of Petaluma, CA antiques store owner and designer Michelle McCauley;

31 The home of Neal and Linda Vitale in Los Angeles, California;

32 l The home of Peg Schrader;

32 c The home of Robert and Laurie Weiner in Ventura, California;

32 r The home of Dawnea Adams;

33 The home of Griselle and William Fiss;

34 al The home of Robert and Laurie Weiner in Ventura, California;

34 bl The home of Dawnea Adams;

34 r The home of Liza and Michael Price;

35 a The home of Dawnea Adams;

35 b The home of Peg Schrader;

36–53 The home of Griselle and William Fiss;

54–63 © Mark Lohman/The home of Nancy and Rick Chace;

64–71 The home of Dawnea Adams;

72–83 © Mark Lohman/The home of artist Erin Anderson and her husband Dan;

84–93 The home of Robert and Laurie Weiner in Ventura, California;

94–105 The home of Neal and Linda Vitale in Los Angeles, California;

106–115 The home of Petaluma, CA antiques store owner and designer Michelle McCauley;

116–127 The home of Liza and Michael Price;

128–137 © Mark Lohman/The home of Nikki and Jeff LaBelle;

138–149 The home of Peg Schrader;

150–159 © Mark Lohman/The home of Amy and Dave Chalmers;

160–170 The home of Barbara and Bruce Gray;

173 The home of Liza and Michael Price;

176 l The home of Barbara and Bruce Gray;

176 c & r © Mark Lohman/The home of Nikki and Jeff LaBelle.

BUSINESS CREDITS

Dawnea Adams
IG: @dawnea_adams
Wip100 Productions Inc
Agoura Hills, CA 91301
Pages 15 a; 32 r; 34 bl; 35 a; 64–71.

Erin Anderson
Artist
www.erinandersonart.com
Pages 3; 8–9; 17; 21 l; 22 a; 24 r; 72–83.

Griselle and William Fiss
Cosy Rose Cottage
www.etsy.com/shop/CosyRoseCottage
Pages 13 l; 15 b; 23 al & br; 27 a & br; 28; 30 l; 33; 36–53.

Barbara and Bruce Gray
IG: @cottagewhite
Pages 7; 13 r; 14 bl; 16 r; 23 bl; 160–169; 170; 176 l.

Nikki and Jeff LaBelle
Susie Holt
Designer
IG: @susie.holt
Pages 29 l & r; 128–137; 176 c & r.

Michelle McCauley
Summer Cottage Antiques
www.summercottageantiques.com
Pages 14 br; 21 c & r; 24 l; 25; 30 br; 106–115.

Liza and Michael Price
Lizabeth K. McGraw of Tumbleweed & Dandelion
Interior designer
www.tumbleweedanddandelion.com

Gabriel Perez of LA Sofa Design
www.lasofadesign.com
Pages 13 c; 16 l; 19 al; 20; 23 ar; 34 r; 116–127; 173.

Peg Schrader
IG: @1925cottagebungalow
Pages 1; 5; 14 al & ar; 16 c; 19 ar; 24 c; 30 ar; 32 l; 35 b; 138–149.

Linda and Neal Vitale
Janet Lohman
Interior designer
janet@janetlohman.com
Pages 4; 10–11; 19 b; 26; 31; 94–105

Robert and Laurie Weiner
The Pink Porch Ventura
www.thepinkporchventura.com
www.facebook.com/thepinkporchventura
IG: @thepinkporchventura
Pages 12; 22 b; 29 c; 32 c; 34 al; 84–93.

INDEX

Page numbers in *italics* refer to the illustrations and their captions.

ACKNOWLEDGMENTS

Thanking all the people who make a book possible is something I always look forward to doing, because without them, quite simply, the book would not see the light of day.

First and foremost, it takes the whole team at Ryland, Peters and Small and CICO Books to bring my visions into beautiful books, and this one is no exception. Warmest thanks to senior commissioning editor Annabel Morgan, editor Sophie Devlin, senior designer Toni Kay, art director Sally Powell, creative director Leslie Harrington and production manager Gordana Simakovic. I am much more appreciative than a simple "thank you" can express, so at the risk of being labeled sentimental (which, by the way, I think is a good thing), I want you to know that I love you all for making me look better than I am for the past 15 years (and, hopefully, the next 15!)

Clearly, the homeowners who allowed us to photograph their homes are right up there at the top of the list as well. Heartfelt thanks to Dawnea Adams, Erin and Dan Anderson, Nancy and Rick Chace, Amy and Dave Chalmers, Griselle and William Fiss, Barbara and Bruce Gray, Nikki and Jeff LaBelle, Michelle and Scott McCauley, Liza and Michael Price, Peg Schrader, Linda and Neal Vitale and Laurie and Robert Weiner.

Another huge thank you goes to designer Lizzie McGraw of Tumbleweed & Dandelion for her wonderful contributions, unfailing creativity and enthusiasm, and for always looking after me and making me feel at home. Jonathan Fineman, thank you for spoiling me with the many exquisite dinners you prepared. And, of course, to Mark Lohman for always delivering beautiful photography for all the books and magazines we have worked on together over the past 15 plus years. Thank you, Mark—your creativity is on full display on every page.

With love, always.

CINZANO